GW00459320

Guilty Men

PETER OBORNE AND FRANCES WEAVER

WITH A FOREWORD BY PETER JAY

THE AUTHORS

Peter Oborne is Chief Political Commentator at the *Daily Telegraph*. He was previously political columnist for the *Daily Mail,* the *Spectator* and the *Sunday Express*. He is also the author of *The Triumph of the Political Class* and *The Rise of Political Lying.*

Frances Weaver is a freelance writer and researcher who has written for *The Week* and is a former columnist for *Standpoint* magazine.

ISBN No. 978-1-906996-43-7

© Centre for Policy Studies, September 2011

Printed by 4 Print, 138 Molesey Avenue, Surrey

CONTENTS

DEDICATION

This pamphlet is dedicated to all those men and women who worked with clear mind and steady purpose to keep Britain out of the Eurozone and thereby salvage our national independence, pride, and prosperity – only to be insulted and derided as cranks, little Englanders, buffoons, racists, maniacs, extremists and xenophobes.

FOREWORD

Britain emerged in 1945 from World War II exhausted and impoverished, but proud, self-confident and secure in its belief that it could and should remain ultimately free to make its own independent decisions about how it engaged with neighbours, friends, allies and others in negotiating the challenges of the post-war world. The war had been fought to preserve that final independence; and becoming part of another country was not remotely part of anyone's agenda, left, right or anywhere else.

Looking back we felt deep pride in the achievements of the long struggle – from the defeat of the Armada by way of Marlborough's defeats of Louis XIV's armies, Chatham's strategy in India and North America, Nelson's and Wellington's defeats of Napoleon and Churchill's defiance of Hitler – to preserve that independence in the face of threats to create a continent-wide despotism on the European mainland and to impose its power on Britain. The traditional foreign policy of counter-balancing any over-mighty threat by alliances and military strength had once again kept us free, free to act as we – and from 1700 our more and more democratically chosen governments – thought best.

Looking back, too, we cherished a long political and cultural tradition which had nurtured a gradual and mainly non-violent transition to greater rights and freedoms for the individual citizen, to widening democracy, to the impartial administration of justice and, eventually, to a new priority for social as well as individual justice. The ideas of Milton, Locke, Tom Paine, John Wilkes, Adam Smith, Burke, Lord John Russell, Gladstone, Bentham, John Stuart Mill, Shaftesbury, Lloyd George, Keynes and Beveridge were milestones along a path of political development bringing us to a new dawn.

Looking forward we faced formidable economic and political challenges; but at least we believed we knew what needed to be done. The United Nations to keep the peace and restrain aggressors, Bretton Woods' World Bank and IMF to foster a prosperous global economy, Marshall Aid to enable Europe to recover from war and build an increasingly open economy, NATO to confront the threat of Soviet expansionism, independence for India and eventually for the rest of the old Empire transformed into a voluntary Commonwealth, a National Health Service and decent welfare: these all seemed enlightened and hopeful signposts to a better and more rational future, purged of the no longer tolerable barbarities of the previous world.

What no one would have predicted was that over the next half-century and more Britain, mainly guided by its most solemn and sacred institutions, led all too often by its governing élite, would set about surrendering those very freedoms, that precise independence, bequeathed to us by the wisdom and courage of the past great leaders and by the fortitude and self-sacrifice of generations of our ordinary ancestors.

Now most of Britain's laws are made in Brussels. How this happened is a story of overriding historical importance, which has yet to be fully and truthfully told.

This book tells the most recent chapter in that story with a clear eye, sparing few blushes and sketching with rare insight the pathology of mind, a kind of group dementia, which progressively blinded those who should – and could – have known better to the nature of the betrayal they were perpetrating.

They were in most cases both able and sincere. They may in some cases have had unhealthy incentives of reward and esteem; but they were not in any crude sense in the pay of a foreign power or animated by some new alien fanaticism. They just did not understand what they were doing.

In choosing the title of their book from that famous earlier study of national betrayal by the nation's élite, the authors of this book have chosen well. Like the appeasers, those who after 1950 worked to deliver their country into the hands of a foreign power – and the particular institutions in which they served – were not individually wicked or vile, though there was indeed something diabolical about the combined arrogance and dirty tricks deployed by the Europhile establishment against anyone who refused to profess the new faith.

It was, my father constantly told me, an exact re-run of the appeasement period in the 1930s when dissent was greeted with suffocating ostracism and personal calumny, reminiscent of the fate of religious non-conformists in earlier times. It recalled too the treatment, at least on the left, of any who did not at least pretend to support CND.

Its spokesmen became past masters of a special kind of double-speak, fudging of all facts and ducking all issues, what Kipling had earlier called "the truthful well-weighed answer that tells the blacker lie". This later reached its epiphany in Edward Heath's endless promises to Parliament that joining the EEC could never jeopardise British independence.

What the élite were doing needs to be explained against a proper understanding of what the European project — "building Europe" — was really about. A myth has been developed and propounded during and since the 1980s, especially beloved of the German leader Helmut Kohl, that it all started from the natural and laudable desire to make any repetition of Europe's pre-1945 history impossible. So, it was about replacing the nationalism of the larger European powers, Germany above all, also maybe France and Britain, with an international union within which war would be impossible, a mini-version indeed of the popular argument in the late 1940s for world government.

But that is a retro-fitted version of history. In fact the whole, "never again" imperative of post-war policy was already fully expressed in the political and economic institutions of the UN, IMF, World Bank, GATT and then Marshall Aid, the OEEC and, in the face of the post-war Soviet threat, NATO. "Europe", in the guise of the Coal and Steel Community, Euratom and the Common Market, had a quite different inspiration, conceived and propagated by the great French diplomat and technocrat, Jean Monnet.

I met him at a small lunch in 1952 in Paris hosted by William Hayter of the British Embassy for my father, then a member of the Labour Opposition's front bench Treasury team. I was 15 and kept my mouth shut, but my ears open. I have never forgotten what I heard. For, it was the truth about the European strategy which he had devised and sold to French political leaders.

France was humiliated by the fact that its representatives were no longer treated by other nations in the way they once had been. Only super-power diplomats were taken seriously. To recover this prestige and standing France must become a superpower like America and Russia with a continental economy to support a continental industrial production and tax base sufficient to deploy or threaten the military might that alone delivers diplomatic weight.

Europe must be welded into such an instrument, by implication, though this was not spelt out, to be dominated and guided by the especially civilised leaders and diplomats which France alone could produce. This could only be achieved gradually and by indirection, as he said, "by zig and by zag" circling round the walls of full political union as the United States of Europe until finally the walls of old-fashioned nationalist sentiment collapsed in favour of a new focus of national unity, Europe itself.

The fundamental purpose of this enterprise could not have been further from the spirit of the post-1945 new dawn and its emphasis on multilateralism and the down-playing of pre-1939 style power politics in the name of the glory and grandeur of successful nations in a kind of political Olympic Games in which only one top dog could win gold.

This was an ethos directly opposed to the positive-sum game of post-1945 internationalism seeking to replace national rivalry with rule-based collaboration. It was a direct route back to that world, but under a new flag, that of "Europe" (whether or not Greater France would have been a more candid name). It was Bonapartist, even if with a twentieth century face.

To me then and since this was deeply shocking – reactionary and dangerous, learning none of the lessons of the previous half-century. It made me a sceptic of "European" political pretensions for good – I voted "No" in 1975 – while strongly in favour of liberalising trade and payments within Europe and beyond.

An acid test of what is truly liberal and what, by contrast, is mega-nationalism on a continental scale is given by attitudes to the admission of Turkey to the EU. To an internationalist of liberal inclinations, it would be a welcome demonstration that Europe is not defined by race, colour, creed or geography, but by a sincere wish to extend free exchange between peoples as far and as fast as may be negotiable with new countries and areas, no more than an advance instalment of a benign globalisation reunifying the human race so long blighted by separate development and mutual dread.

To a Euro-nationalist (otherwise a French Third Empire-builder such as Valéry Giscard D'Estaing) to admit Turkey would be a dangerous dilution of the purity and cohesion, and therefore the strength, of Europe as an ethnically, religiously, geographically and culturally homogeneous political actor and as a new power in the world. It is a dead give-away of what should be an unacceptable purpose.

The groups who have most particularly betrayed Britain's independence and support for a multinational shared management of our real global problems in favour of merging Britain into an old-fashioned power-seeking country called "Europe" have been mainly motivated by muddled thinking and immature sentiment. The number of people who in their early youth just thought of Europe as a nice place for culture, sunshine, wine and skiing and made this the foundation of their

vi

view of the political and economic architecture being imposed on the UK is pathetic and shocking.

More insidious yet was the great "middle ground" confidence-trick, whose real pioneer was the late great – and he was a very great and talented journalist – Peter Jenkins. Other hugely distinguished journalists like the late Hugo Young of the *Sunday Times* and *Guardian*, and Philip Stephens of the *Financial Times,* built on the foundations which Jenkins laid; and deployed Jenkins' model of politics week in and week out for decade after decade.

This proceeds by, first, insisting that political choices are necessarily arranged along a one-dimensional spectrum from left to right. Secondly, anything near the ends of the spectrum is called "extreme" – and by implication weird and mad – and anything in the middle is correspondingly "moderate" – and by implication sensible, reasonable and sane. The third step is to stipulate that support for European unification and Britain's total involvement in it is in the middle ground – and therefore, QED, moderate, sensible, sane – and so right.

Despite the accident of the horse-shoe model of the French constituent assembly in 1789 at Louis XVI's Versailles whence the terms left and right derive, there is absolutely no objective basis for arranging political choice along this one-dimensional spectrum. Still less is there any reason to regard support for "Europe" – more especially a Europe modelled on the Bonapartist tradition – as in any sense a centrist or moderate position. For me it smacks much more of the long European tradition of nationalism, protectionism and power-politics designed to promote the ascendancy of the chosen nation. As such it belongs, if anywhere, at the right end of any such spectrum.

Jenkins, Young and Stephens believed what they wrote and wrote with great skill and frequency. But they naively swallowed the childish sleight of hand that made "Europe" an international cause, to be contrasted with "little England" scepticism, simply because Europe was "abroad" however much its architects were in the business of building a mega-nation and however much the sceptics were in the business of making a multinational world.

In the foreign service, of which I had a brief experience, the mechanism of betrayal was more directly self-interested and vested in institutional structures. New recruits are required on entry to select two easy (i.e. west European) languages or one hard language (e.g. Arabic, Chinese, Russian) to learn. This quickly leads to the service being divided into a series language-based clubs who graduate from learning the language, to serving in the area, to sympathising with its concerns, to becoming finally advocates and supporters of its causes.

The only countries which are unrepresented in this pattern, since new recruits cannot opt to learn English, are the English-speaking countries, especially Britain, the old Commonwealth and the United States. I have written elsewhere about the baneful effect this has on Anglo-American relations.

I had a deputy in Washington who, it seemed to me, not merely believed that building "Europe" should be the overriding goal of British policy, but also that, since relations with "Europe" and with the US were a zero-sum trade off, weakening relations with the US – which was easy from Washington – was just as desirable as strengthening relations with Europe – which was more difficult when on the far side of the Atlantic. So he did the former.

This club structure is at the root of the old jokes about how the job of the Foreign Office is, like the Ministry of Agriculture to look after farmers, to represent the interests of foreigners. It interacted with a generational shift whereby after Suez, when President Eisenhower cut off the Eden government's military adventure at the knees simply by putting pressure on sterling in the foreign exchange markets, the young Turks in the F.O. concluded that they as diplomats and possibly Britain as a medium-sized power would have more influence in collaboration with similar sized – and smaller – powers in Europe.

Though they were a smallish minority of the office and there were plenty who disagreed, the minority came to exercise a decisive influence on foreign office policy from about 1960 onwards. Influence is of course the base currency of diplomats. It often seems that it matters not a jot whether or not Britain gains or loses from some projected agreement so long only as we emerge with "enhanced influence".

It also often seems that it is a currency one can never spend, a reserve on which one can never draw, because one must always be accumulating yet more of it at whatever cost to our here-and-now interests. The great way to gain influence, it is supposed, is to swallow some radically unfavourable outcome.

Thus, almost uniquely in British political history, it came about that Britain's government contained a civil service group, the foreign service, who had a vested interest – the enhancement of their own influence – which was at no point connected to the interests of the people who employed them.

From 1960 onwards, through the Macmillan and Wilson and Heath bids to join the EEC, the Thatcher acceptance of the massively centralising Single Market, John Major's deluded belief that Maastricht safeguarded British independence when indeed it crossed the Rubicon of Brussels majority rule and finally Tony Blair's hankering to join the Euro, from which Gordon Brown's defiance alone rescued us, the foreign office was the decisive force driving British policy on Europe.

Political parties might have other ideas in opposition. They frequently did. But once back in Whitehall the sweet seduction of high level diplomacy unhinged Prime Minister after Prime Minister and some, but not all, Foreign Secretaries.

This book analyses too how other pillars of the British establishment, such as the CBI, was for a while corralled into the "pro-Europe" camp. I should say a word about the BBC, which also comes in for severe censure from the authors.

Not only was I for a dozen years a loyal and believing member of the BBC news and current affairs team from 1990-2001. I was its Economics Editor during the exact period of some of the coverage of the debates about the Euro of which the authors most strongly complain. During the run-up to the Maastricht Treaty, which I regarded with more or less total horror, I broadcast many times on TV and radio, news and current affairs, hewing to what I perceived as an impartial BBC line, but doubtless letting the slip of my scepticism show from time to time.

I had and have no doubt that the BBC's coverage was markedly tilted towards a favourable, view of "Europe" and of the Euro project. This was not, I thought, some heavy top-down diktat from senior management.

It was indeed not even intentional. It was just a deeply ingrained cultural tilt in the sub-conscious associations in the minds of young people, many of them highly intelligent, who had grown up thinking Europe was a nice place for a holiday and assuming that doubt about its political ambitions must spring from a small-minded even narrower focus on British – or English – nationhood. They had simply never been exposed to the broader more serious issues, as already discussed here.

It was however possible, with a bit of determination, to make major current affairs films, e.g. for Panorama and the Money Programme and the 1992 Election Specials, exploring those wider and deeper issues. I did it and with full-hearted co-operation from immensely talented producers, who were often fascinated by hearing questions asked and perspectives offered which they had simply never considered before.

This did not remove the problem that the overall impact of BBC coverage was manifestly slanted to a Europe – and Euro-favouring posture, though I would still claim that the main nightly News coverage of, for example, the exit from the Exchange Rate Mechanism on 16th September, 1992, was scrupulously correct. If it shed any visible tears at all that night, they were the tears of a crocodile, mine.

Finally, while I agree with much of what the authors say about the *Financial Times* and just about all of what they say about the CBI in the high periods of ERM- and Euro-mania, I must enter a word of dissent on behalf of the two greatest economic journalists of this time, Sir Samuel Brittan and Martin Wolf. Though Samuel explored almost every aspect of the "Europe" question from a range of perspectives from sympathetic to doubtful he was consistently clear-eyed in dissecting the delusions and dangers of large currency blocs which suppress the all-important shock-absorbers between economies, namely changeable exchange rates. Martin repeatedly and devastatingly exposed the basic economic fallacies on which the dream of monetary union among multiple countries of uneven competitiveness was based, notably yet again on the very day I am penning these words in September, 2011.

My only complaint was that neither of them fully saw that it was the very dysfunctionality of the Euro which was its chief attraction to the Bonapartists. They could safely rely upon it to cause the periodic acute crises which then supplied the political context for the next great leap forward in Euro-centralisation, edging ever closer to one country, be it Third Empire or Fourth Reich, enshrining Monnet's City on the hill from which French diplomats could go forth with German cheque books in their baggage to strut their hour upon the world stage.

Peter Jay
10 September 2011

Peter Jay has been Economics Editor of The Times, *Ambassador to the USA and Economics Editor of the BBC.*

1. INTRODUCTION

"A happy 10th anniversary Emu – Europe's currency union has been a remarkable success", headline to a leading article in the *Financial Times*, 26 May 2008

New Year's Day 2002 was a day of joy and triumph for the British left/liberal élite. One of its most cherished objectives had been attained: the European single currency had come into existence.

The *Financial Times* – one of the longest standing supporters of European Monetary Union – waxed lyrical:[1]

> The new currency is a triumph of political will over practical objections. Its physical launch is a testament to a generation of visionary leaders who pursued a dream, often against the grain of public opinion.

---

[1] Leading article, *Financial Times*, 2 January 2002. It is curious that the subtitle to this article does not appear on the *FT* website.

TUC general secretary John Monks noted that it would be "disastrous" if the UK Government failed to follow suit and hold a referendum on the single currency.[2] Peter Mandelson took the opportunity to warn that "staying out of the Euro will mean progressive economic isolation for Britain."[3]

It was a moment of celebration for the BBC, whose already fragile sense of perspective collapsed. The BBC forgot its duty of impartiality. It abandoned its statutory responsibility to distinguish between reporting and comment. And it was nakedly contemptuous of its mass British audience.

Here is Paul Mason, now economics editor of Newsnight, reporting from Maastricht on 3 January:[4]

> As the midnight hour approached, a giant inflatable tree blossomed into life. For once the Ode to Joy seemed exactly the right tune.

Today Programme presenter Jim Naughtie, in France on 1 January, spoke of:[5]

> ...a sense of occasion, a genuine excitement, a sense of peculiar new notes, a sense of change in the air especially among young people, a sense of breaking away from the past.

---

[2] John Monks, "New Year's Message", December 2001. See www.tuc.org.uk/the_tuc/tuc-4128-f0.cfm

[3] *Sunday Mirror*, 18 May 2003.

[4] As detailed in Minotaur Media, *The BBC and "Europe": Introduction of the Euro survey, January 1 – 8, 2002.*

[5] Ibid.

Naughtie lapsed into mystical language, strikingly similar to the words used in St John to describe one of the central mysteries of Christianity: "The arrival of the currency that the fathers of modern Europe dreamed about are symbols now made flesh."[6]

Greg Wood on the Today Business News interviewed Jean-Claude Trichet, governor of Bank of France (and now president of the European Central Bank). There were few lucid, sceptical, or intelligent questions about the internal contradictions of the new currency. Rather, M Trichet was asked to give his personal views about whether Britain should follow the French example and join. When M Trichet responded that the arrival of notes and coins would have "a decisive influence on the people of the UK and in Europe", Wood left the remark unchallenged. Nor was there any effort to ask anything awkward or controversial in what was effectively a naked piece of single currency propaganda.

This pattern was to be repeated. Here is Today Programme reporter Michael Buchanan in France:[7]

> Walking up the Champs Elysée with its sparkling Christmas lights, towards that most French of national monuments, the Arc de Triomphe, you get the feeling that this is a country very much at ease with this latest engagement with Europe.

Buchanan went on, in a loaded remark apparently aimed at British euro-sceptics:[8]

---

[6]   Ibid.

[7]   Ibid.

[8]   Ibid.

For people here, the Euro has got little to do with loss of sovereignty or European superstates. It's about money, pure and simple.

This was the message that the pro-Euro campaigners wanted. The Euro was a simple and innocent matter, with no deep consequences. Now – with several Eurozone countries in collapse – we know how false that prospectus was, and how misleading was the BBC's institutional complacency.

The BBC Charter, with its demand for neutrality and professionalism, was broken again and again in those early days of the Euro. Guidelines on balanced reporting were repeatedly ignored. Reasonable doubts about the Euro were severely underplayed. Some reporters failed to distinguish between normal New Year revelries and specifically Euro-related celebration. This meant that the sense of excitement was over-emphasised. Italy, for example, did not hold any celebrations to mark the arrival of the Euro, but this was barely mentioned by the BBC.[9]

The BBC was metropolitan in its approach, concentrating its reporting resources on the large European capital cities where support for the Euro was likely to be strongest, while neglecting country areas and the small towns where so many Europeans still live – one reason why BBC vox pops on 1 January 2002 were weighted five to one in favour of the Euro.[10]

The BBC's reporting sent out one overall message: that the Euro project would bring benefits and it was only a matter of time before the UK would join. No wonder one BBC journalist,

---

[9] As reported by Minotaur Media tracking, Ibid.

[10] Twenty vox pops of those strongly in favour of the new notes and coins, compared to four strongly negative vox pops, Ibid.

Jonathan Charles, later mused about the beginning of European Monetary Union in 1999:[11]

> Even now I can remember the great air of excitement. It did seem like the start of a new era. For a few brief days I suppose I and everyone else suspended their scepticism and all got caught up in that euphoria.

This BBC coverage should be seen as part of a wider and more significant national pattern as many mainstream British institutions were subverted to serve the aspirations of the pro-Euro camp. At the start of this century, a massive effort was launched by senior figures of the British political class to drive this country into the Euro. Had this campaign been successful, it would have meant economic devastation and political humiliation for this country.

The title of this short work – *Guilty Men* – is drawn from the book written in the summer of 1940 as Britain awaited Nazi attack in the wake of Dunkirk. The intention of that famous book was to call to account the architects of the policy of appeasement who had betrayed the people of Czechoslovakia at Munich in 1938. It was written by three journalists – Frank Owen of the *Evening Standard*, Peter Howard of the *Sunday Express* and Michael Foot, later to become Labour Party leader and an advocate of Britain's withdrawal from the EU.

Our intention is to reveal the methods, and call to account the politicians and propagandists who sought to tie the fortunes of

---

[11] Quoted by Peter Hitchens, *Mail on Sunday*, 5 September 2010. Jonathan Charles, who now works for the European Bank of Reconstruction and Development, today insists that the general tone of his reporting of the Euro for the BBC was sceptical, and that he frequently warned of troubles that might lie ahead.

Britain to the single currency. We will remind them of what they said and did at the time, of the fabrications they produced, and how they unfairly trashed the reputations of those with whom they disagreed.

This is not an empty exercise in score-settling. Even today, with large parts of Europe reduced to economic devastation, sections of the British political directorate are still refusing to come to terms with the slow but inevitable collapse of the single currency. In defiance of the evidence before their eyes, former cabinet minister and European Commissioner Peter Mandelson and former Prime Minister Tony Blair continue to speak of British membership at some future date.[12] Influential political commentators like Will Hutton of the *Observer* and Philip Stephens of the *Financial Times* still defend the Euro project. Meanwhile the Foreign Office and Whitehall establishment urges that Britain should write out cheques for billions of pounds, at a time when Britain is facing severe spending restrictions, to sort out the financial devastation caused by the Eurozone.

Catastrophe Averted

Just imagine we had joined the Euro – as so many members of the political class urged. We – like Portugal and Greece – would have been unable to confront the consequences of the 2008 financial crash. The credit boom of the 2000s would have been worse, the excesses of the property market more extreme, the subsequent crash far larger and more drastic. Denied the advantages of a floating exchange rate and monetary freedom

---

[12] "Peter Mandelson facing questions about claim UK will join euro", *Daily Telegraph*, 1 December 2008; Tony Blair in an interview with the BBC Politics Show, 26 June 2011.

(control of our own interest rates was derided as 'meaningless' by Nick Clegg in 2001),[13] the international markets would never have funded our deficit. Interest rates would have hurtled upwards, and the European Central Bank and International Monetary Fund would now be dictating British economic management.

This terrifying state of affairs demands a radical reassessment of recent British political history. The conventional wisdom goes as follows: in the mid-1990s, the Conservative Party went mad. It became unfit for office, paralysed by its obsession with Europe and in particular the single currency. In its place, Tony Blair's New Labour became the natural party of government: sane, pragmatic, pro-Euro, responsible.

According to this version of events, a number of leaders – especially William Hague and his successor Iain Duncan Smith – led the Conservative Party down a cul-de-sac. It talked too much about a matter which did not interest voters: the EU. There were men of good sense and moderation available in the shape of Ken Clarke, Chris Patten and Michael Heseltine. But the fin de siècle Conservative Party, according to this version of events, made the suicidal decision to ignore their advice. Only with the rise of the modernisers, led by David Cameron and George Osborne towards the end of the 2000s, did this madness end; and the EU finally closed down as a subject of debate.[14]

Here is a different story: William Hague, Iain Duncan Smith and others showed extraordinary prescience and moral courage in

---

[13]   Letter dated 24 November 2001, published in *Prospect*, January 2002.

[14]   For a good example of the accepted wisdom see Tim Bale's much praised study, *The Conservative Party: From Thatcher to Cameron*, Polity, 2010.

spelling out the dangers of the single currency. Far from being mad – as their many critics maintained at the time – they were sane. And not only were they right about the impending failure of the Euro: they were right for the right reasons.

In contrast, the analysis of the Euro supporters was hardly sane and reasonable. Rather, the British political directorate was overcome by what might be regarded as a collective mania. Many of our most senior politicians were determined to drive this country into a disastrous economic system – an outcome which was only averted by the courage of a handful of unfashionable politicians and the stolid good sense of the British people as a whole.

It is time to reclaim the reputation of key figures in that national debate ten years ago. William Hague, Margaret Thatcher, John Redwood and others were mocked at the time. Nor should it be forgotten that Sir John Major – so often criticised by Euro-sceptics – insisted on the opt-out from European Monetary Union. But they all played glowing roles. Their reputation needs to be redeemed. All of them – as well as other unfashionable and sometimes derided figures such as the Tory MP William Cash, the *Sunday* and *Daily Telegraph* journalists Christopher Booker and Ambrose Evans-Pritchard, Trevor Kavanagh of the *Sun,* the businessmen Malcolm Pearson and Rodney Leach, the campaigners Dominic Cummings and Brigadier Anthony Cowgill and many, many others – deserve our thanks, and the apologies of their antagonists. Having studied the record, we have failed to find a single public argument by Gordon Brown against the Euro. Nevertheless, there is no question that his opposition from inside government was an essential factor in keeping Britain out of the single currency.

There were also villains. These came in two forms. The most important are institutional: the CBI, the BBC and the *Financial*

Times. Each of these organisations lost integrity by permitting itself to become the propaganda arm for the pro-single currency movement.

The standard of debate was often debased. Many of the individuals arguing the merits of the single currency showed a very troubling lack of personal scruple and integrity. They had no hesitation in resorting to personal attack and cheap innuendo in order to discredit Euro-sceptic campaigners. They have shown little remorse. None has apologised.

The purpose of this pamphlet is to recall the errors, falsehoods and libels uttered by the advocates of the single currency as we enter a defining stage of the long-standing national debate of the UK's connection with the European Union. We urgently need to learn the lessons from the debate of the 1990s and 2000s.

2. XENOPHOBES AND MADMEN

"On the pro-Euro side, a grand coalition of business, the unions and the substantial, sane, front-rank political figures. On the other side, a menagerie of has-beens, never-have-beens and loony tunes with only two things in common: their hostility to Europe and their unpopularity in Britain." – Andrew Rawnsley, *The Observer*, 31 January 1999

The most powerful tactic used by those in favour of the Euro was to maintain that their own beliefs were inspired by logic and rational thinking, as opposed to Euro-sceptics, who were driven by dark and irrational motives. Take Diane Coyle, former economics editor of the *Independent* (and now vice chair of the BBC Trust). In 1999 she stated:[15]

> The defenders of sterling are, in the main, a group of elderly men with more stake in their past than in our future. They clothe their gut anti-Europeanism and Little Englandism in the language of rational economic argument.

---

[15] *Independent*, 8 April 1999.

There are a number of observations to be made about this attack. Firstly, it was untrue. There were plenty of people who were sceptical about the benefits of joining the Euro who weren't elderly, or, for that matter, men. And there were elderly men who happened to be pro-Euro. But why Diane Coyle's assumption that defenders of sterling were hiding their real intentions behind rational economic argument?

We suggest that those within the pro-Euro consensus were often reluctant to engage with the complex debates on the single currency, and preferred to be lazy and use provocative language and imagery because it proved such a useful way of excluding an opponent from the fight. Looking at the articles of a handful of journalists in various papers at the time – Hugo Young in the *Guardian*, Andrew Rawnsley in the *Observer*, David Aaronovitch and Johann Hari in the *Independent* and Philip Stephens in the *Financial Times* – it is easy to spot the crude, marginalising tactic of referring to anyone on the other side of the argument as a crank. Aaronovitch led the way:[16]

> But it has to be said (and this is one of the features of this debate), that I am not passionate about it [the Euro]. For me, it's a currency, not a crusade. I cannot discover within myself more than a fraction of that partisan heat that seems to infuse the bodies and minds of the "no" campaigners. I do not believe that it will be the end of the world if we don't enter the Euro soon, whereas many of the no-sters really seem to think that the Euro is the fifth horseman of the Apocalypse.

---

[16]   *Independent*, 5 July 2002.

Here are some of the insults thrown at euro-sceptics: they were cast as "men of intellectual violence" who were consumed by "last-ditch extremism"; who wore a "veil of middleness" which was "self-deceiving";[17] who uttered one "seductive, slippery soundbite" after another;[18] who "stoked the phobic fire and sceptic propaganda so high";[19] whose anti-Europeanism had an "insidious potency"; who were weighed down by the "baggage of phobia, sentiment and illusion";[20] and who represented the "paradigm of menace and defeat"[21] – all phrases used by the late Hugo Young in the *Guardian*, and simply because they merely weren't sure about the benefits of joining the Euro.

In the *Independent,* Johann Hari – who has since been exposed as a fabricator – claimed that "there's so much poison pumped into the British psyche about the EU that it's worth stopping for a moment to realize how incredible this is." Hari referred to the "angry flecks of euro-scepticism", described euro-sceptics as "foaming", wrote in an especially disgusting phrase about "all this euro-sceptic pus", while accusing the Tories of "Hun-bashing, frog-thrashing xenophobia". Hari (like David Aaronovitch, a winner of the Orwell Prize for political journalism[22]) asserted that "the anti-Europeans want to hum 'Land of Hope and Glory' as they nuke the British economy."[23]

---

[17]   Hugo Young, *The Guardian*, 7 January 1999.

[18]   Ibid, 10 June 1999.

[19]   Ibid, 10 June 2003.

[20]   Ibid, 17 June 1999.

[21]   Ibid, 10 February 2000.

[22]   Following revelations of plagiarism, Hari has since returned the Orwell Prize.

[23]   These quotes are drawn from the *Independent*, of 19 March 2007, 4 June 2005, 15 April 2005, 21 April 2004 and 9 May 2003.

When these euro-sceptics – whose "default mode" according to Hugo Young was "raging fury"[24] – suffered any sort of defeat in the political realm then they would become "enraged"[25] or so "apoplectic"[26] that they would almost "choke on the foam of their own outrage".[27] If, however, they were lucky enough to celebrate any victory – and this was of course down to luck, rather than talent or being on the right side of the argument – then they would become "gleeful" with delight.[28] There was a constant tone of menace and madness – any defender of sterling, in short, became a pathetic caricature, a monster or Dr Evil of the currency world.

Both Hugo Young and Philip Stephens (in the *Financial Times*) casually referred to the "vortex" that the Conservative Party was finding hard to escape from in its discussions about the Euro.[29] This seems such a strange and startling way in which to view a debate about the single currency, and one that says something about the mindset and paranoia of the writers themselves.

But there does come, occasionally, a hint of sympathy. The euro-sceptics were being pushed by forces beyond their control, by emotions they couldn't manage, by personal desires that couldn't be restrained. It's not their fault, they just can't stop their "bilious hatred of all things European from bubbling to the

---

24 Ibid, 10 June 1999.

25 Ibid, 17 June 1999.

26 Ibid, 10 June 1999.

27 Ibid, 6 June 2000.

28 Diane Coyle, *The Independent*, 8 April 1999.

29 Hugo Young, *The Guardian*, 6 May 2003 and Philip Stephens, *Financial Times*, 3 September 1999.

surface", according to Rawnsley.[30] Euro-scepticism "courses like a virus through the veins of the Conservative Party', claimed Philip Stephens. "Defying all remedies, the fever will not abate".[31]

To read this you'd think that writers like Stephens experienced a genuine fear that euro-scepticism could be contagious. The *Financial Times* columnist was certainly at pains to point out its toxicity though – arguing that "the poison of Black Wednesday has curdled scepticism into phobia".[32] All of this disturbing imagery – the bilious hatred which bubbles, the virus, the fever, the curdling – was used to scare people off of the idea that the consensus in the media and press could be faulty. And again there appears the notion that euro-sceptics are evil seducers, who tempt you into wrong by tricking you or infecting you with their virus.

At best, silky seducers; at worst conquering anti-Euro "forces"[33] or armies that march to the "drum-beat"[34] of the pound whilst on a "crusade" that is "messianic",[35] and who have, indeed, "stormed the citadel".[36] David Aaronovitch took this deliberate misrepresentation of euro-sceptics as menacing troops to its logical conclusion when he wrote:[37]

---

[30] *Observer*, 7 July 2002.

[31] *Financial Times*, 10 October 1997.

[32] Ibid, 3 September 1999.

[33] Hugo Young, *Guardian*, 1 July 1999.

[34] Ibid, *Guardian*, 10 June 1999.

[35] Donald Macintyre, *Independent*, 3 June 1999 and 18 May 1999.

[36] Philip Stephens, *Financial Times*, 3 September 1999.

[37] Independent, 18 March 1999.

Echoes of the Europhobes' golden age were to be heard on the streets of Riga this week, when veterans of the Latvian legion of the Waffen SS observed their annual get-together, drinking beer and reliving old massacres.

Few of Aaronovitch's target audience would take the time to look behind the Nazi imagery to the baffling assumptions hidden there: that British euro-sceptics were rabid, nationalistic Europe-haters who fought against the Nazis in World War Two, while simultaneously viewing the time that German fascism was at its height as a "golden age". Most would be happy to lazily enjoy the connection between euro-sceptics and their natural fascist, anti-semitic, genocidal partners in Latvia.

In the argument over the Euro, for those in the consensus there was no real opposition – there were just those within it, the establishment, who were reasoned and logical "grown-ups"; and those without, who weren't worth listening to.

Day after day there was a concerted effort made by leading politicians and journalists to crudely label the Conservative Party as a doomed collection of untouchables and fanatics who were striding stubbornly towards their own destruction. Tony Blair led the way with vindictive and personal attacks. In his conference speech of 1999, he claimed the Conservative party was made up of "the uneatable, the unspeakable and the unelectable... Under John Major, it was weak, weak, weak. Under William Hague, it's weird, weird, weird. Far right, far out... The more useless they get, the more extreme they get."

In the same speech he emphasised the menacing and sinister impact that the "forces of conservatism" have had in Britain. It is these forces, so he claimed, that were behind the opposition to women's suffrage, and it is these same forces that were at work in 1999:

> The forces of conservatism allied to racism are why one of the heroes of the 20th Century, Martin Luther King, is dead. It's why another, Nelson Mandela, spent the best years of his life in a cell the size of a bed.
>
> And though the fact that Mandela is alive, free and became President, is a sign of the progress we have made: the fact that Stephen Lawrence is dead, for no other reason than he was born black, is a sign of how far we still have to go.
>
> And they still keep opposing progress and justice.

Then Blair went on to talk about those opposed to the single currency, those "Europhobes" who attempt to "blindfold and dull" us into backing away from Europe. The unmistakable implication was that those forces of conservatism behind the racist murders of Martin Luther King and Stephen Lawrence, and the imprisonment of Nelson Mandela, were the same forces that motivated those who were against joining the single currency, forces that were especially prevalent within the Conservative Party.

Three Case Studies in the Politics of Personal Destruction
The attacks were made not just on the Conservative Party. They were made on individuals as well. The following three case studies show how personal they could be.

William Hague, the extremist

William Hague was said to be out-of-his-depth, overshadowed by obsessive euro-sceptic and euro-phobic bigwigs of the party, and pushed to further isolation over the EU out of desperation.

Here is Hugo Young's insulting analysis:[38]

> William Hague, who occupies a position from which some faint vestige of veracity was once expected, sprays generalised terrors that long ago stopped even attempting to connect with the truth.

Two weeks later Young continued:[39]

> The new plausibility of apocalypse makes Hague's own half-way-out extremism seem more acceptable, and ensures that he will never be caught saying a single thing in favour of the European Union.

These attacks by Hugo Young can only have been a deliberate misrepresentation of William Hague's position. The Tory leader of course emphasised his support for the European Union many times during his leadership (and since): and after all, Hague also fought the 1999 EU elections on the slogan "In Europe, not run by Europe", and in the late 1990s the Tories only ruled out joining the single currency for the duration of that Parliament. His statement in February 2000 clearly encapsulates the Conservative Party's stance towards the EU:[40]

---

[38] Hugo Young, *Guardian*, 10 February 2000.

[39] Ibid., 24 February 2000.

[40] BBC News Online (www.news.bbc.co.uk/1/hi/uk_politics/650295.stm), accessed 2 June 2011.

Every sensible person agrees that Britain should be in the European Union. The Conservative Party took us into Europe and the Conservative Party will keep us in Europe. The real debate in British politics is not about Europe – in or out – as Tony Blair wants to pretend. The real debate is about the Euro – in or out – and Tony Blair knows he is losing the argument.

In a speech at the CBI conference in 1997 he argued that:[41]

Unlike the ERM, the single currency exists for all time. British business could find itself trapped in a burning building with no exits... if the nightmare of our experience in the ERM teaches us anything it is not to steer by the siren voices of a supposed consensus, but to exercise independent judgement of a cool head.

He went on to the set out his reasons for saying No to the Euro in July 1999:[42]

...keeping the pound means we can run the British economy in the interests of British business and British jobs. Monetary sovereignty, like any other sovereignty, is not the ability to do whatever you want; but it is the ability to make your own choices. With our own currency, interest rates can be set specifically for our own economic conditions, to reflect the supply and demand for credit in this country. That is a huge advantage for any country, but particularly in Britain where the large number of

---

[41] As reported by Michael Harrison in the *Independent*, 11 November 1997.

[42] Article in the *News of the World*, 9 July 1999.

home owners with mortgages makes our economy particularly sensitive to changes in interest rates. Having the freedom to adjust Britain's interest rates relative to the rest of the world can help us offset temporary economic imbalances in a reasonably benign way. Depriving ourselves of that policy tool would force us to rely on drastic and destabilising adjustments to budgetary policy. The alternatives are inflation or unemployment.

This was logical, reasoned argument whose wisdom has been borne out by events. But it was too much for pro-single currency journalists and politicians to admit that a clever, reasonable man like Hague had objected to entering the Euro at that time out of logic and rational consideration. So they sought to assert that he was a euro-sceptic for less worthy reasons.

Here is Philip Stephens in the *Financial Times*:[43]

The young Tory leader is not a spiteful or a stupid man. I find it hard to believe that he set out to cut adrift Messrs Heseltine and Clarke. And yet that outcome was at times inevitable when he sought the endorsement of party activists for his opposition to Europe's single currency. Immaturity is the kind explanation.

However, Hague would come to look like a moderate compared to the picture painted of Iain Duncan Smith.

---

[43] Philip Stephens, *Financial Times*, 9 October 1998.

2. Iain Duncan Smith, the Fascist.

To the supporters of the euro, Iain Duncan Smith was a sinister, hysterical fanatic with a dark past. He was described as a "dogmatic extremist"[44] with links to the "rabid right"[45], heading a "hardline coalition of European right-wingers".[46] Lord Skidelsky, biographer of John Maynard Keynes and briefly a Tory treasury spokesman, accused Duncan Smith of a "hysterical" brand of "anti-intellectualism".[47]

Hugo Young reasoned that, to most people, Duncan Smith's Conservative Party represented a "sect with an obsession that divides it from mainstream business and political life."[48] According to Johann Hari in the *Independent*, Iain Duncan Smith was "an obsessive anti-European headbanger."[49]

There were several smear campaigns made against him in the pro-Euro tabloids – most commonly in the *Daily Mirror*. Oonagh Blackman, writing for that paper in August 2001 in an article headlined "IDS and the Euro Loons", uncovered Duncan Smith's "links to a string of extreme anti-Europe groups", saying he was trying to "shake off claims that he was a magnet for racists and other extremists."[50] As evidence she cited his ties with euro-sceptic ginger groups Conservative Way Forward, Conservatives

---

[44] Hugo Young, *Guardian*, 10 January 2002.

[45] "IDS and the Euro loons: his links to the rabid right", Oonagh Blackman, *Daily Mirror*, 28 August 2001.

[46] "KKK joins IDS: Tories unite Europe hard right", Oonagh Blackman, *Daily Mirror*, 2 October 2001.

[47] As reported in the Daily Mirror by Paul Gilfeather, 17 October 2001.

[48] *Guardian*, 10 January 2002.

[49] *Independent*, 9 May 2003.

[50] Oonagh Blackman, *Daily Mirror*, 28 August 2001.

Against a Federal Europe and the European Foundation, as well as a speech he gave at an event for the Campaign for an Independent Britain. Two months later Blackman wrote an article headlined "KKK joins IDS – Tories to unite Euro hard right" in which she stated that "The man second-in-command of the racist Ku Klux Klan in Britain has joined the Tories. Bill Binding, 76, a former candidate for the British National Party, is a fan of Iain Duncan Smith."[51]

It is only after further reading that we learn that Duncan Smith was, in fact, furious at the membership and had issued a statement saying: "We will have no truck whatsoever with racists or those who use race as part of a political creed. I loathe the Ku Klux Klan, I loathe all that they stand for, I loathe all those organisations that use race hatred."[52] So for those whose habit is to read a newspaper by glancing at the headlines the impression is that the Conservative Party formed an alliance with the American racist far-right in the name of the single currency.

Blackman then goes on to add that Duncan Smith is:

> ...said to have met Alleanza [Alleanza Nazionale, the Italian right-wing political party] boss Gianfranco Fini, who once described Mussolini as 'the greatest statesman of the century'. Tories deny any deals have been done but one source said the US atrocities were being used to 'sneak in' the change.

Having met someone does not indicate any significant relationship whatsoever. Claiming that Duncan Smith was using 9/11 as a means of distracting people from his forging ties with

---

51 Oonagh Blackman, *Daily Mirror*, 2 October 2001.

52 Ibid.

right-wing Black Shirts was a terrible accusation to make, and looks especially short-sighted considering that it was a Labour aide who was guilty of believing September 11 was a good day to bury bad news.

Through these kind of vague and misleading slurs journalists like Blackman and Hugo Young were able to gradually misrepresent Duncan Smith and create the grotesque caricature that he was a secret fascist.

Lord Owen, Enoch Powell and Oswald Mosley.

But the most loaded assaults were reserved for the former SDP leader and Labour foreign secretary, David Owen – perhaps because he was seen as a turncoat. David Owen was even compared to Enoch Powell and Oswald Mosley, despite his liberal background and his dedication to social democracy and equality.

The pro-Euro camp felt special hatred for David Owen. The former foreign secretary's position could scarcely have been more moderate. His campaign group New Europe was in favour of the European Union, but against the euro. This position inspired especial scorn. Here is the reaction of Hugo Young:[53]

> The think-tank Owen is setting up is strictly for people 'whose hallmark is a lifetime of commitment to the European Union'. He doesn't want anything to do with those with 'a long track record of scepticism'...
>
> This ambition overlooks the unsheddable burden of history. It's rather too late to be removing from the

---

[53] Hugo Young, *Guardian*, 7 January 1999.

anti-Euro case the decades of straightforward anti-Europe sentiment that lie behind it. The depth of this sentiment long ago defined the language in which the anti-EU argument is now always conducted. It's as if no other language would be understood.

As time goes on, this reaches ever further towards the kind of last-ditch extremism that allows no merit in any aspect of 'Europe'. The mind-set created by 18 years of Thatcherism, and the incessant anti-Europe propaganda in most of the tabloid press, together leave no space for the subtle distinctions Lord Owen says he hopes to make.

It is worth pondering the implications of Hugo Young's verdict: it defines anyone opposed to the single currency as a Europhobe. He is arguing that Europe is a black and white issue: you are either for it or against it. Young wrote that this opposition to the single currency sought to place Britain on the fringe of Europe, or even "over the edge into a different world".[54] David Owen, once a person "of measured judgement" to Young, was now displaying his "lurid plumage of alarm".[55]

So David Owen too was an "extremist". However, David Aaronovitch would take this one step further in an article for the *Independent*, in which he placed David Owen in the same category as Enoch Powell and Oswald Mosley. These "three great lost leaders", considered Aaronovitch, had a lot in common:[56]

---

[54] Hugo Young, *Guardian*, 7 January 1999.

[55] Hugo Young, *Guardian*, 10 February 2000.

[56] David Aaronovitch, *Independent*, 13 February 1998.

All three were once held in the kind of regard by some of their contemporaries that most politicians never experience. All three were said to possess rare intellectual gifts, to be men of destiny, to be prophets standing above party and beyond compromise, to be in direct contact with the soul of the nation. And, in Powell's words, to be odd men out... As they failed, all three turned to some form of sectionalism, to ancient nationalism and – in the case of Powell and Mosley, to racism. It is interesting to note that what is at stake for Owen is "the whole history of this country", not its whole future.

One must assume that Aaronovitch puts these three politicians together intentionally, and with the purpose of marginalising Owen in the way that Powell and Mosley have been marginalised. Aaronovitch may say that we should be careful to note the differences between the three, but then why compare him to Powell and Mosley at all? The use of Powell and Mosley is one that implicitly seeks to create a false and damaging link between opposition to the Euro and racism.

3. THE CAPTURE OF THE INSTITUTIONS

"We could stop listening to the assorted maniacs, buffoons, empire-nostalgists, colonial press tycoons, Save The Groat anoraks and Yorkshire separatists of the Europhobe movement, and prepare for our earliest feasible entry into the euro. Once in the Euro we would immediately reap the benefit of our competitiveness, our goods competing – in eternity (which in economics is quite a long time) – on a level playing field." – David Aaronovitch, *Independent*, 2 February 2001.

Here was the strategy: to create the widespread impression that those arguing against the Euro were mad, racist or xenophobic. This story was for a time extremely successful, and convinced even some Conservatives that they should drop opposition to the Euro as a political campaign.[57]

---

[57] See, for example, the fascinating claim made by Tim Montgomerie, editor of Conservative Home and a former Central Office official and chief of staff for Iain Duncan Smith. According to Montgomerie, David Cameron's strategy chief Andrew Cooper used to urge entry

However, the demonisation of key individuals would never have gained traction without the collaboration of certain British institutions. The most important of these was the BBC.

The BBC

Few organisations apart from Parliament, the armed forces and the judiciary stand so clearly for what it is to be British as the BBC. The state-owned broadcaster is at the heart of our national life, and should above everything else represent the British values of tolerance, fair-mindedness and decency.

Sadly the BBC made little attempt to live up to these essential values while the battle for the Euro was being fought around the turn of the century. Instead it allied itself with the left/liberal élite, and framed the debate in a way that the supporters of the Euro were bound to win. The methods used were insidious. BBC broadcasters tended to present the pro-Euro position itself as centre-ground, thus defining even moderately euro-sceptic voices as extreme, meaning that they were defeated even before they had entered the debate.[58]

---

to the Euro on pragmatic grounds: "Not because it was morally right, not because it was economically sensible, not because the Euro was popular with voters but because it would show the Conservative Party had changed." However, Andrew Cooper denies this account, saying that Montgomerie "attributed views to me that I do not hold and have never held". See *Daily Mail*, 16 February 2011.

[58] The observations which follow are based in part on the thorough work carried out by Minotaur Media Tracking, a monitoring group run by a former BBC producer and a research sociologist, who conducted regularly surveys into the BBC's coverage of the EU and the euro, including two which covered the 1999 EU elections and the General Election in 2001.

It is highly improbable that this alliance between the Euro supporters and the BBC reflected any kind of conscious decision or arrangement. It was simply that the high-minded attitudes of BBC producers and reporters meshed only too easily with those of the pro-Euro pressure groups. However it was achieved, this alliance between the state broadcaster and the pro-Euro camp was of profound political importance.

Through programmes such as Today, World at One, Newsnight, Question Time, Any Questions, Panorama and Ten O'Clock News, the BBC enjoys a quasi-monopoly of broadcasting news coverage. This brings with it a heavy responsibility of impartiality, one which is set out in statute and freely acknowledged by the BBC itself.

But the corporation failed to give equal amount of coverage to the two sides debating the merits of the single currency and of further integration into the EU, consistently favouring those who were pro-euro. Here is just one example: in the nine weeks between 22 May and 21 July 2000, the Today programme on Radio 4 featured 121 speakers on this topic: 87 were pro-Euro compared to 34 euro-sceptics. These euro-sceptics provided 34 interviews and 21 soundbites, whilst the pro-Euro camp provided 72 interviews and 40 soundbites. The case for the Euro was represented by twice as many figures, interviews and soundbites than the case against.[59]

This unfairness would have been less of an issue if those euro-sceptics who were granted media access were given an adequate amount of time to defend their position and state their reasons for favouring sterling. This was not the case. The euro-sceptic position was too often covered through a

---

[59] *The BBC and Europe: 'Today' Survey, 22 May − 21 July 2000*, conducted by Minotaur Media Tracking for Global Britain.

paradigm of deep, "explosive" splits within the Conservative Party rather than the merits of the policy argument.

To a certain extent, these so-called rifts were generated by the BBC. The Corporation concentrated to a disproportionate extent on a new self-proclaimed Pro-Euro Conservative Party led by John Stevens MEP. Despite its name, this party had no connection at all with the official Conservatives. Furthermore it only managed to gain 1.4% of the vote in the 1999 EU elections, failing to win a single seat. Nevertheless it was granted extensive exposure on the BBC, always creating the strong impression of a disastrous Tory split on Europe – and often on extremely significant days.

For instance, comments by John Stevens prefaced an interview with William Hague on Today on the 8 June 1999, two days before the EU elections. The matter of the Pro-Euro Conservatives dominated this interview. A change in topic only came with the attempt to connect the Conservatives with Alleanza Nazionale (the neo-fascist Italian party) – something that William Hague strongly denied immediately. This alleged connection between William Hague and Italian fascists had also led the World at One the day before, despite laborious denials.[60] These insinuations were so disturbing that they could

---

[60] Minotaur Media Tracking made transcripts of BBC programming for their paper, Reporting of the Elections to the European Parliament on UK Terrestrial Television Services and BBC Radio 4 for Global Britain, which can be found on their website: http://globalbritain.org/BBC.asp (accessed 10 June 2011). It is significant that outside voices both at the time and since confirmed the general Minotaur analysis. For example the crime novelist PD James, a former governor of the BBC, accused the Corporation of 'skewing the picture' over Europe. In an interview with the Spectator in August 2000 the Baroness said of BBC reporters that "I feel they are pro-Europe. I'm sure of that." Here is the verdict of a leading BBC figure, Michael Buerk: "What the BBC regards as normal and

cause maximum damage during election week despite their spurious nature.

John Stevens was granted an extraordinary amount of respect by the BBC. His claims that his party could split the Conservative vote and lead to the latter polling under 25% were featured twice in a news bulletin on BBC Radio 4 on 9 May 1999.[61] One month later, the Conservatives picked up 35% of the vote.

The contrast between the generous coverage accorded by the BBC to Stevens' Pro-Euro Conservatives and the meagre coverage for much more legitimate and far larger euro-sceptic groups is telling. The United Kingdom Independence Party, which was to poll an impressive 7% in the EU elections, was virtually ignored by contrast with the Pro-Euro Conservatives. Similarly, prominent euro-sceptic members of the Labour party, such as Frank Field and Austin Mitchell, seem also to have been under-

---

abnormal, what is moderate or extreme, where the centre of gravity of an issue lies, are conditioned by the common set of assumptions held by the people who work for it. These are uniformly middle class, well-educated, living in north London, or maybe its Manchester equivalent. Urban, bright thirty-somethings with a pleasing record of achievement in a series of institutions, school, university, BBC, with little experience of — and perhaps not very well disguised contempt for — business, industry, the countryside, localness, traditions and politicians. The Guardian is their bible and political correctness their creed." Standpoint, April 2011. Similarly, Peter Sissons, the long-standing BBC news anchor, says this: "In my view, 'bias' is too blunt a word to describe the subtleties of the pervading culture. The better word is a 'mindset'. At the core of the BBC, in its very DNA, is a way of thinking that is firmly of the Left." Sissons adds that the BBC regards the European Union as 'a good thing'. Peter Sissons, When One Door Closes, Biteback Publishing, 2011.

[61] Ibid.

represented. Furthermore their rebellion against the party line wasn't represented as a 'split' in the way that John Stevens's Pro-Euro Conservatives disagreement with William Hague was.

This meant that the Liberal Democrat leader Paddy Ashdown and Labour leader Tony Blair were both granted an important advantage. They were able to conduct interviews with the BBC which focused on the policy details and substantive reasons why they supported joining the single currency. In contrast, William Hague had to spend a large amount of his time, especially during the crucial week before the election itself, discussing overblown splits and other marginal issues, missing the opportunity to inform viewers of the reasons for opposing Eurozone entry.

Indeed, pretty well any figure, however marginal, implausible or dated, would do to fuel this BBC-sponsored narrative of Tory 'splits' on Europe. A letter to The Times from, among others, Sir Julian Critchley, who had already stood down as an MP, expressing doubts about the Conservative policy, made headline news on BBC news broadcasts during the election period.[62]

The BBC would also use partial and misleading language when discussing the Conservative position on the euro. Thus BBC presenters labelled William Hague's rather mild opposition to the so-called change-over plan – an expensive attempt to prepare business and Government for single currency membership – "hard-line".[63]

Another problem with BBC language was the way in which the value of the pound was addressed – almost always as high,

---

[62] Ibid.

[63] Presenter on BBC Radio 4 'World at One', 1 June 1999, Ibid.

despite it being in a weak position compared to the dollar, and rather than commenting on the weak value of the Euro against sterling. This language was accompanied by unchallenged claims that millions of jobs would be at stake if we did not join the Euro – accompanied by a failure to do justice to positive reports about foreign investment.[64] In fact, the UK at the time – despite being outside the Eurozone – was enjoying record levels of foreign investment. But when reports of record foreign investment did appear, they tended to appear low on the list of headlines, with the BBC downplaying positive official figures in favour of scare stories. When the Today programme addressed record investment levels in July 2000 in their news bulletin, they did so only after first covering a story about a leaked comment from the ambassador to Japan expressing concerns about investment in the UK.[65] But the figures from the Office for National Statistics are evidence enough that these concerns were grossly exaggerated by the BBC: inward investment was at a record high of £54 billion in 1999, and would increase by £22.7 billion to £77 billion the next year.[66]

The Financial Times

Almost as central to the pro-Euro cause was the *Financial Times*. The *FT* lacked the wide reach and mass audience of the BBC, but brought to the pro-Euro campaign something nearly as important. It was the acknowledged voice of the City of London and the business community.

---

[64] Ken Livingstone on the Today programme on 17 June 2000 and Sir Ken Jackson of the AEEU on 30 June 2000, according to *The BBC and Europe: Today survey' from 22 May – 21 July, 2000.*

[65] 5 July 2000, Today programme, Ibid.

[66] ONS, http://www.statistics.gov.uk/downloads/theme_economy/MA4 2000.pdf (accessed 28 June 2011).

Like the BBC, the *Financial Times* made special claims for impartiality, fairness and high standards of integrity. Like the BBC, the *Financial Times* abandoned its impartiality during the debate over the Euro. Under the editorships of Richard Lambert and Andrew Gowers, the paper flung itself headlong into the pro-Euro camp, embracing the cause with an almost religious passion.

Sceptical voices rarely appeared in the paper. The *FT* ramped up stories which helped the pro-Euro case, minimising the counter-argument. For instance, it copied the BBC in presenting William Hague's reasoned objections to the Euro in terms of a narrative of Tory rifts.[67] It gave credence to the scare stories from the pro-Euro camp that foreign investors would pull out of Britain unless we joined the single currency, while failing to give comparable prominence to reports showing that inward investment was being maintained.[68] In one article that addressed the record investment Britain was experiencing in July 1999 it commented that "Britain's non-membership of the Euro has not deterred investors" whilst swiftly adding the caveat: "although there could be problems if it seemed unlikely to join."[69]

---

[67] For an example of the *FT* prioritizing the Tory "rift" story over the mainstream argument, see the front-page story, 'Clarke scorns Hague's ideologues', 29 December, 1999.

[68] The *FT* leader of 27 June, 2000 is an excellent example of an unbalanced opinion piece which uncritically swallows the heavily partisan pro-European line on inward investment. Or see 'Sterling's part in Rover's death', 29 April, 2000 which contains the controversial claim that "worst difficulties now faced by manufacturers would not have happened within the euro-zone".

[69] Brian Groom, *Financial Times*, 15 July, 1999.

As we have seen, Philip Stephens, the most powerful political voice of the newspaper, entirely lost objectivity on the euro. He regarded British entry not merely as desirable, but inevitable, while trashing the reputations of politicians, above all William Hague, who opposed the idea. The same applied, though to a lesser extent, to the newspaper's editorial columns. Abandoning scepticism, they were devoted to a diet of pro-single currency advocacy.[70] On 2 January 2002, the FT waxed poetic:[71]

> After decades as a dream, 10 years as a plan and three as a virtual currency, the Euro has arrived. The prosaic details of the introduction of Euro notes and coins conceal its historic significance. The new currency is a triumph of political will over practical objections. Its physical launch is a testament to a generation of visionary leaders who pursued a dream, often against the grain of public opinion. The reputations of Helmut Kohl, the former German chancellor, and Francois Mitterrand, the former French president, have faded. But their achievement, together with that of Jacques Delors, the former European Commission president, who

---

[70] For telling examples see the *FT* leaders from 15 October 1999, in which the paper called for Tony Blair to make "a firm commitment" to membership of the single currency and the leader from 27 September 1999 calling for Tony Blair to get off of the fence in favour of the euro; 16 June 2000 when the paper argued that the Government "should be preparing the country much more vigorously for possible entry"; 6 June, 2000 when it argued that "the Euro debate should be won on the quality of arguments in favour of British membership"; 24 November 2001, which listed the benefits and greater influence Britain would have within the euro; and 7 January 2002, when the FT said the Government "must come out fighting for a 'yes' in the referendum", if and when it is called.

[71] 'Small change, giant leap', *Financial Times*, 2 January 2002.

masterminded the project, is beyond dispute. That the Euro has arrived is also a tribute to the dedication and common sense of central bankers and treasury officials across Europe.

This lyricism was to continue long after its problems started to become manifest. "European monetary union is a bumble-bee that has taken flight," enthused an *FT* leader in May 2008, while the fatal booms in Ireland and elsewhere were already starting to collapse. "However improbable the celestial design, it has succeeded in real life."[72] The following month the *FT* hailed EU enlargement as a "fantastic success".[73] Study of the editorial and news pages shows an extraordinary lack of scepticism even about the accession of peripheral countries like Greece and Ireland.

Here is the reaction of the *FT*'s respected Lex column on 8 January 2001, as Greece signed up to the euro:

> With Greece now trading in euros, few will mourn the death of the drachma. Membership of the Eurozone offers the prospect of long-term economic stability.

The *FT* was equally adrift when Ireland joined the Eurozone. The paper gave two of its star economic reporters, Ed Crooks and John Murray Brown the task of examining the evidence that the Irish boom could get out of control. They concluded: "providing that danger in the housing market can be avoided, the euro-

---

[72] "A happy 10th anniversary Emu – Europe's currency union has been a remarkable success", *Financial Times*, 26 May 2008.

[73] "Engaging the EU – Europe's leaders must sell their success story more clearly", *Financial Times*, 19 June 2008.

sceptics hoping for an Irish disaster may yet be disappointed."[74] Interesting here is the insulting assumption made by *FT* writers that euro-sceptics were "hoping" for an Irish disaster. No evidence was provided for this insulting assertion that euro-sceptics were emotionally involved in the outcome, rather than soberly warning of trouble ahead.

At least Crooks and Murray Brown were prudent enough to qualify their optimistic assessment of the Irish economy. Not so another writer commissioned to write for the *FT*, Dermot O'Brien, who dismissed all warnings about the future. "Although strong growth has produced some strains," declared O'Brien, "these need to be seen in perspective. They are not so strong as to seriously risk the economy's buoyant prospects."[75]

The creation of the Euro was the most important financial story of the age, and the *FT* got it hopelessly wrong. It ceased to be a sober-minded reporter of financial affairs, becoming instead the enthusiastic propaganda arm of what was, at bottom, a political project.

Consider, for example, the reports sent back to London by the paper's Brussels bureau chief Lionel Barber. His reports, with their insistent pleading that Tony Blair should sign Britain up to the euro, suggest that Barber lost that necessary detachment from his sources that all good journalists must retain if they are to tell their readers the truth. Take this example: "Britain will not take a leading role without joining the first circle [i.e. signing up to economic and monetary union]," wrote Barber on 4 July 1998. "This means meeting Europe's expectations and joining EMU in 2002-3."

---

[74] *Financial Times*, 17 July 2000.

[75] *Financial Times*, 23 August 2000.

Or consider Barber's report from 3 December 1997:

> Since the Labour government entered office six months ago, it has pretended that delayed entry into economic and monetary union would be virtually cost-free for Britain. A single Gallic thrust has exposed the policy as threadbare.
>
> In the words of Dominique Strauss-Kahn, France's finance minister, monetary union is a marriage. And as he observed with undisguised relish on Monday night in Brussels: 'People who are married do not want others in the bedroom.'

Quite so. But there is a mystery about these reports from Lionel Barber. Even though he worked for a financial newspaper, he consistently ignored or downplayed the economics. Instead the *FT* Brussels chief concentrated on what he saw as the risk of political isolation facing Britain, thus failing to report on what was in due course to turn into the real story: impending financial catastrophe. Lionel Barber, who was reflecting his newspaper's policy, is today the Editor of the *Financial Times*.[76]

But in general the *FT* was guilty of an historic failure both in its journalistic standards and editorial judgement. For a newspaper with the *FT*'s pretension to authority in financial matters, this can be regarded as nothing short of a disaster.[77]

---

[76] One honourable exception to the *FT*'s support for the Euro stands out: the paper's economic writer, Martin Wolf who was cautious about the euro.

[77] The *FT*'s lapse was not unusual: its judgement was equally at fault over Britain's membership of the Exchange Rate Mechanism in the early 1990s; it opposed the Falklands war in 1982; and it endorsed Neil Kinnock as prime minister in the 1992 general election.

Today, the FT's grave problems with Europe persist. In recent months it has been regularly scooped on the unfolding Euro story by its main rival, the *Wall Street Journal*, which has provided far more comprehensive and lively coverage. Could the poverty of the *FT* coverage of the euro-debacle in part reflect the emotional commitment of far too many of its editorial staff to the EU cause?

It is time that the *Financial Times* explained why it got the single currency so wrong for so long. So too should its political columnist Philip Stephens apologise to the Conservative politicians who so presciently warned against the single currency ten years ago – and who he mocked for their pains. In particular, he should apologise to William Hague, whose brave warnings have been amply vindicated by events.

The CBI

There has always been an argument, and sometimes a bitter one, about who exactly the Confederation of British Industry (CBI) represents. The great majority of British firms are small businesses, with only a few employees.[78] But the inner councils of the CBI have traditionally been dominated by a handful of large corporations. The interests of these very large corporations and very small businesses are by no means identical. One key difference concerns the European Union. Large companies can be fond of the EU because they see it as a source of lucrative contracts, and they have the resources to shape the directives that flow out of Brussels to suit their

---

[78] For example, in 21004 the CBI represented around 200,000 businesses. 90% of these were small- and medium-sized enterprises. See http://business.timesonline.co.uk/tol/business/article418797.ece.

interests. Small companies tend to dislike big government because they see it as a source of regulation and tax.

By the mid 1990s, the usual group of large companies were firmly in control at the CBI. Furthermore they had got the director-general they wanted, in the shape of the impeccably connected Adair (now Lord) Turner, a banker who later went on to become chairman of the Financial Services Authority and who is now chairman of the Government's Committee on Climate Change. No conventional wisdom, it can be said, is too conventional for Lord Turner. He and his allies set about selling the message that business backed the Euro.

Sir Colin Marshall, the former British Airways CEO who was then CBI president, warned of "the tide of Euro-scepticism which threatens to wash over the country", and for good measure of "wilder anti-Europe positions being taken up in some quarters [which] are not just daft, they are dangerous". His predecessor, Sir Bryan Nicholson, went yet further, arguing that "the voice of moderation has been swept aside by emotion".[79]

These fears were needless to say reflected in the *Financial Times*, which informed its readers that such remarks represented "widespread concern in the business community" at the spread of extreme euro-scepticism, and that "many felt they were seeing their worst fears confirmed".[80]

In April 1997 an article appeared on the front page of the *FT* which stated that the CBI's President's committee, its main policy-making body, had put out a consultation document which

---

[79] As reported in "Business leaders lambast the Euro-sceptics: 'Voice of moderation has been swept aside – we have to work with our European partners", *Financial Times*, 23 April 1997.

[80] Ibid.

contained·three options for the organisation concerning their policy on the single currency:[81]

- That sterling should join in the long term;
- That it should join at the 1999 launch;
- That it should join after a short time observing the new currency's performance.

Not one of these options, it should be noted, contemplated the possibility that Britain should stay out of the Euro altogether. A "senior" industrialist was quoted as saying that "some powerful people, notably Niall Fitzgerald of Unilever and Sir David Simon of BP, are pushing us to say that the UK should be in from the start." Sir Colin Marshall claimed that "the general direction of opinion is clear" in the business community, with the majority favouring entry into the euro.[82]

Meanwhile those business organisations that tried to tell a different story were undermined, marginalised, and punished. A particularly sinister story concerns the Institute of Directors and the treatment of its then Head of Policy, Ruth Lea, who challenged the CBI/FT/BBC consensus that business supported the euro. Following government pressure Lea was targeted. Stories were put about that she was mentally unstable, a claim that was palpably false. Eventually she was thrown out of her job and the IoD became a supporter of the euro.[83]

---

[81] "CBI is poised to back European single currency: Tory supporter Paul Sykes launches £1m campaign against EMU", *Financial Times*, 23 April 1997.

[82] "CBI chief attacks anti-Euro group", *Financial Times*, 24 June 1998.

[83] For a fuller account see Peter Oborne, *Spectator*, 29 May 2004.

Enter Brigadier Cowgill

Every so often a small man steps forward to play a part in the great events of his time. This was the destiny of Brigadier Anthony Cowgill. Few people today have heard of Tony Cowgill, a professional soldier who served on Montgomery's headquarters staff after D-Day, and played an important role as India prepared for independence in 1947. Later he served as chief industrial engineer for Rolls Royce.

Cowgill stood for everything that was alien to proselytisers for the pro-Euro camp. He had a deep and varied experience of life. He had hard-nosed experience of industry, rather than an abstract specialisation in economic theory. Above all he worked on the basis of raw, empirically provable data rather than attaching himself to a grand narrative. This old soldier's most significant contribution to British history came when he was already retired, when he produced his dramatic intervention in the battle over the single currency.

In 1994, as the pro-single currency movement was starting to rumble, the CBI published the result of a survey which claimed to show that 84% of industry backed British membership of the Euro – potentially, an incredibly valuable propaganda tool for the pro-single currency campaign. To Brigadier Cowgill's experienced eye, however, it looked distinctly fishy.

And when he came to examine how the CBI had reached these figures, he discovered that the business organisation had not carried out a scientific survey of the views of its member firms. Indeed the CBI had sent out questionnaires to only 624 companies, of which just 206 had replied. Of those 206 only 59 – 28% – had positively supported the single currency.[84]

---

[84] For this account of how Brigadier Cowgill exploded the claims of the CBI we are relying heavily on Christopher Booker. See in

However, a further 56% of respondents had been more lukewarm, without being hostile to the single currency. Only once they were added in was the CBI able to make their claim that a majority of members were in favour.

In the summer of 1998 the CBI announced that it was to stage a fresh poll of its members, to be supervised by Bob Worcester (now Sir Robert) of MORI. Professor Anthony Cowgill asked Worcester for a private meeting, in which he challenged the famous pollster that it would be "unprofessional" to give his name to the survey. Sir Robert was faced with a dilemma. Either he could go ahead with a genuine, random poll. But that might not produce the results the CBI sought. Or he could produce a rigged poll – but that would be disreputable. In the end the CBI withdrew from its proposed poll. However, the *FT* published details of its own poll taken by MORI, which found that 63% of British businesses were in favour of joining the Euro. The CBI instead used this poll to claim that the majority of British business supported the single currency.[85]

Senior CBI members then staged their counter-attack. It was around this time that Business for Sterling was founded. Essentially a breakaway organisation from the CBI, it was initially backed by the Institute of Directors and the Federation of Small Businesses, and its founder Lord Marsh explained his reasons for creating the group, saying:[86]

> It's assumed business is for the Euro just because the CBI says so, but that is not true. In that sense,

---

particular Christopher Booker, "Why the CBI has called off its Europoll", *Sunday Telegraph*, 30 August 1998.

[85] *Financial Times*, 28 September 1998.

[86] Reported in the *Financial Times*, 12 June 1998.

the CBI irritates me and irritates a lot of other people in business.

Business for Sterling produced a rival survey, carried out by ICM in March of the next year. ICM found that the earlier *Financial Times* claim that "a majority of UK companies" favoured British participation in the Eurozone to be palpably false.[87] As the *Financial Times* reported (to its credit), among businesses polled only 41% supported Euro entry, and around 59% of UK businesses were opposed to the Euro.[88]

There was a crucial difference between the Business for Sterling survey and the previous surveys: businesses with ten employees or fewer were allowed to take part – businesses that the MORI survey for the *FT* excluded. Nick Sparrow, managing director of ICM, noted that including smaller businesses was crucial, as most of Britain's four million or so businesses employed less than ten people.[89]

By excluding businesses with ten or fewer employees, and by weighting their survey in terms of company size, the earlier surveys were allowing those large multinational corporations – who were much more likely to favour the single currency – to represent the British business community as a whole. The CBI leadership used these surveys to bolster their own position and argue that British business was in favour of the euro. Adair

---

[87] "Most favour early entry but ready: a survey by MORI for the FT finds 63% of British businesses think the UK should join the Euro sooner rather than later", *Financial Times*, 28 September 1998.

[88] "Poll shows 60% of UK businesses opposed to euro", *Financial Times*, 31 March 1999.

[89] 'Poll adds heat to euro-debate: New survey suggests that the majority of businesses are opposed to participation in the single currency', *Financial Times*, 31 March 1999.

Turner protested that the rival ICM survey favoured small businesses. But as a group of businessmen who had served as members of the CBI wrote in their letter to the *FT* in April 1999:[90]

> When the CBI claims that more than 90 per cent of the companies it represents are smaller firms, it ill behoves them to argue that polls should be weighted in favour of big business.

Extensive debates over the survey results and the issuing of counter surveys would take place over the following year. But an indisputable reality was appearing every time – that business was divided over Euro entry. The first poll results set out in the *Financial Times* had not reflected this division. Instead a deceptive attempt had been made to assert that business was behind the single currency.

Not until Digby Jones became director-general would the CBI cease to present a picture of solid backing for the euro.[91] In

---

[90] "CBI's policy on Euro should not be over-influenced by larger companies", letter to the *Financial Times*, 14 April 1999.

[91] Note that, like the *FT*, the CBI's failure of judgement on the Euro is not an isolated incident. As Jesse Norman has revealed in his blog ("The CBI has gone Awol on every issue that matters", 1 September 2011): "Its recent record on key issues such as bank reform, the private finance initiative and executive pay is lamentable. On all three it has consistently taken the side of big business against the interests of its smaller members and the taxpayer, and has done so in defiance of the facts... On all these issues the CBI talks small business and acts finance. It could be a huge force for good, fighting crony capitalism and promoting real, competitive, risky, entrepreneurial day's-work-for-a-day's-pay capitalism — the sort that will eventually get us out of this mess. Yet at the moment the CBI seems to prefer the interests of a few big companies and banks to those of the hundreds of thousands of ordinary businesses that make up its membership."

January 2000, Digby Jones would tell members of the CBI that the "sterile" debate over the Euro had damaged companies and that the Confederation would stop promoting entry to the Euro-zone until a referendum were called over the matter.[92] 87.5% of the CBI's leading members, when polled in the following months, stated their approval of this new policy.[93]

Of course this change at the CBI was noted with dismay by the pro-Euro establishment. Over at the *Guardian,* Polly Toynbee articulated this alarm: [94]

> Something has happened to the CBI. It is not the same organisation it once was under the temperate and intelligent leadership of Howard Davies and Adair Turner. It has moved sharply to the right, no longer representing a middle-of-the-road business world, but tugged towards the new extremism and euro-phobia in the Tory party.

---

[92] Reported in the *Financial Times,* 31 January 2000.

[93] Reported in the *Daily Mail,* 21 November 2000.

[94] "The CBI have turned into a bunch of extremists: a once intelligent organisation has been hijacked by rightwingers", *The Guardian,* 29 November 2000. Even the language of Polly Toynbee's column shows the scale of the problem. Merely to express scepticism about the single currency was to be labelled an extremist.

4. SCARE STORIES

"Staying out of the Euro will mean progressive economic isolation for Britain. It will mean fewer foreign businesses investing here, fewer good jobs created and less trade being done with our European partners." – Peter Mandelson, *Sunday Mirror,* 18 May 2003.

The central weapon of the pro-single currency camp was not, however, opinion polls. It was economics. Failure to join the single currency, they asserted, would hamper job creation and bring about over time a breakdown of British commerce and industry.[95]

Once again it was the BBC that supported the scare stories and fabrications put out by the pro-Euro campaigns. One favourite trick of the pro-Euro campaigners was to give publicity to supposed claims by important foreign companies that, if Britain failed to join the euro, they would either pull out of Britain or

---

[95] A selection of quotations illustrating these stories is in Appendix One.

cancel fresh foreign investment. Again and again the BBC would highlight these claims; and again and again the firms concerned would put out denials which the BBC would fail to report.

The problem became so glaring that the campaigning journalist Christopher Booker assembled a dossier of such stories and presented them to the BBC.[96] The tale he tells is so shocking that it is worth recording it in full. Booker here takes up the story:

> The first of five examples I gave the BBC was how, on October 14, 1997, the Today programme reported as the day's top news a claim by Mustafa Mohotarem, the chief economist at General Motors, that his company would move car production out of the UK if the UK did not join the single currency. Although this claim was later trenchantly rejected by General Motors, the BBC did not report its denial.
>
> On December 10, 1997, the BBC highlighted a decision by Toyota to site a major new factory in France. The real reason for this was that Toyota had been offered French government subsidies of around £700 million to locate the factory nearer to continental markets. But BBC presenters and interviewers persistently suggested the main reason for Toyota's decision was the UK's refusal to join the single currency.

---

[96] He reported the BBC reaction in "Sorry is the hardest word for euro-loving reporters at the BBC", *Sunday Telegraph*, 20 January 2000.

On January 28, 1999 the Today programme's business news led on a claim in the *Daily Express*, owned by leading Britain in Europe supporter Lord Hollick, that the Bank of America was to move its European head office from London to Frankfurt because of Britain's refusal to join the euro. When the bank later put out a statement that the report was "completely untrue", the BBC ignored it.

On November 24, 1999 Today reported a *Daily Telegraph* story that three major car companies had warned Mr Blair that they would have to reconsider their investments in Britain if the UK delayed entry to the euro.

Most recently, on February 13, Today reported that the chairman of Sony had warned Mr Blair that "the high pound, plus being outside the euro, threatens future investment in Britain". Sony protested. It was true the chairman had expressed concern over the strong pound, but he had not mentioned the euro. Again the BBC failed to report the correction.

As Booker noted, "no attempt was made to answer the central question I had put to the BBC, asking why it failed to report the subsequent denials of its reports."[97]

These alarmist predictions were part of a pattern of alarmist statements put out by the pro-Euro camp. Failure to join the Euro, they claimed, would cause economic devastation to Britain. The only disagreement was the scope of the damage.

---

[97]   Ibid.

Three million jobs, one million jobs, eight million jobs, 35,000 jobs, 10,000 jobs a month, 150,000 jobs, a job every two minutes: any which way, a desperate state of affairs for the UK if it remained outside of the Eurozone (or eventually withdrew from the EU, which many Euro supporters claimed was the secret ambition of opponents of the euro).[98]

Leading politicians joined in the doom-mongering. Peter Mandelson warned staying out of the Euro would be a disaster:[99]

> The price we would pay in lost investment and trade and jobs in Britain would be incalculable...

Three years earlier he had also warned that:[100]

> As long as we are outside the euro, there is little we can do to protect industry against destabilising swings in the value of sterling.

Ken Clarke endorsed this: "Britain's economy will be damaged if we stay out too long."[101] Cabinet minister Peter Hain warned: "I

---

[98] "Boycotting Euro could cost 3m jobs and £6bn", *Daily Express*, 23 February 1999; "Euro campaigners clash on jobs: Lord Marshall says investors will pull out of Britain but sceptics ridicule claims", *Guardian*, 30 June 1999; "Eight million jobs 'would be lost if Britain quit EU'", *Independent*, 18 February 2000; "Join Euro now, urges car boss: 35,000 jobs at risk in components industry if we stay out", *Observer*, 18 June 2000; "10,000 jobs a month will go unless Britain joins euro, warns Monks", *Independent*, 29 December 2000; "Adopt Euro or lose jobs", *Daily Mirror*, 29 December 2001; "No to Euro costs a job every 2 mins", *Daily Mirror*, 3 January 2003.

[99] "Mandelson warns Blair over Euro", *Daily Telegraph*, 20 May 2003.

[100] Speaking at a Trade Union conference in Belfast, 16 May 2000.

[101] *Independent*, 10 May 2003.

doubt that in the end it is possible to run a sort of parallel currency economy."[102]

Not wishing to be left out of this reassuring cross-party consensus, the Lib Dems' Chris Huhne declared that failure to join the Euro would lead to a collapse of inward investment. Indeed he mocked euro-sceptics who warned that the Irish economy would overheat once it joined the Euro because of low interest rates.[103] On the subject of Ireland he was backed up by the *Independent* economics editor Diane Coyle (now the deputy chair of the BBC Trust). In August 2000, she revealed that a leaked International Monetary Fund report would shortly dismiss the argument "that membership of the single currency has caused a damaging inflationary boom in Ireland that will end in recession."[104] This argument, sniffed Coyle, was "often made by euro-sceptics."[105] In the event, the euro-sceptics were proved completely right.

The great jobs scare

Political columnists joined in with this doom-mongering, creating the strong impression that a failure to join the single currency would lead to a powerless Britain and one that would have no influence in the modern world. "Join the Euro or watch jobs

---

[102] Speaking on Today Programme, 1 January 2002.

[103] Huhne dismissed Conservative euro-sceptic warnings about Ireland thus: "According to Francis Maude, the shadow chancellor, the Irish experience shows the perils of Britain joining the euro. This has become a repeated refrain among the euro-sceptics." But Huhne knew better: "Mr Maude had better watch out, as this may prove to be an embarrassingly premature judgement." Huhne concluded that "Ireland has the sort of economic problems the British should die for." Chris Huhne, *Independent*, 23 August 1999.

[104] "IMF verdict on Ireland to disappoint euro-sceptics", *Independent*, 7 August 2000.

[105] Ibid.

vanish", as Hugo Young gravely warned in *The Guardian*.[106] "The Government will need to move fast after the election to start the process of joining the euro," said John Monks of the TUC. "The alternative is that we pay a heavy price for staying outside, and then pay a heavy price for having to join far too late to have any real say in shaping the euro's future."[107] Lord Marshall, the chairman of Britain in Europe and a former President of the CBI, felt "convinced that inside the single currency, on the right terms, Britain will be stronger in the world, not weaker; our economy and our people will be more prosperous not less; and our future will be confident, not backward looking."[108]

Then there were baseless rumours, like the claim reported by the *Daily Express* in 1999 that Bank America, America's biggest bank, had dropped plans to base its European headquarters in Britain.[109]

There are two central points to be made about these warnings that sterling could not survive outside the euro. The first is that they largely proved misleading. On unemployment, GDP growth and direct investment, the UK has performed markedly better than the Eurozone over the past ten years, though claims that the UK would lose manufacturing jobs at a faster rate than Eurozone competitors have indeed proved true.[110]

---

[106] "Join the Euro or watch jobs vanish. It's Brown's choice: There's one way to bring sterling down, but the government is wilfully blind", Hugo Young, *The Guardian*, 6 April 2000.

[107] Quoted in the *Independent*, 29 December 2000.

[108] "Why we must join the euro: Colin Marshall is launching a campaign for Britain to join the single currency. He explains why Emu is a good thing", *Observer*, 21 March 1999.

[109] "Jobs fear as bank pulls out over euro", *Daily Express*, 28 January 1999.

[110] See Appendix 2 for a more detailed note on UK and Eurozone economic performance over the last decade.

The second is that the techniques used by euro-campaigners were irresponsible and in many cases unscrupulous. We have already shown how pro-Euro columnists would resort to vicious personal attack and smear in order to discredit those who spoke up for sterling. A parallel process took place among pro-Euro reporters.

The pro-Euro marketing campaign, sculpted by Danny Alexander (now chief secretary to the Treasury), was called "Out of Europe, Out of Work". It was essential to construct stories around this central, though false claim. The most terrifying statistic was printed by the *Daily Express* and the *Independent*: inward investment in British manufacturing would be cut by a third, and Britain would lose no less than *eight million* jobs if it pulled out of the European Union. This figure was attributed to research by the National Institute of Economic and Social Research.[111]

On the same day that this statistic graced the national news, NIESR issued a reproachful statement which rejected the "absurd reports" as "a serious misrepresentation". Director Martin Weale went to the lengths of stating that the way facts had been distorted was worthy of Dr Goebbels. Unhappy at the way the findings had been manipulated, he refused to attend the launch of the report, which was supported by Britain in Europe.[112]

---

[111] "8 million jobs in jeopardy", *Daily Express*; "Eight million jobs 'would be lost if Britain quit EU' ", *Independent*; "Quitting EU 'would hurt inward investment' ", *Financial Times* – all 18 February 2000. And "Blair backs warning on jobs toll of quitting EU", *Daily Express*, 19 February 2000.

[112] "Quitting Europe 'would not bring big job losses'", *Guardian*, 19 February 2000.

5. LEARNING THE LESSONS

"I will tell the House the use of recriminating about the past. It is to enforce effective action at the present." – Winston Churchill, House of Commons, 29 May, 1936.

Cognitive Dissonance and the gradual collapse of the Euro

Some members of the pro-Euro camp remain unabashed. Tony Blair, for example, has recently insisted that he still hopes Britain enters the euro.[113] Likewise Philip Stephens at the *Financial Times* resolutely holds to his position, in defiance of all evidence, expert opinion, and indeed common sense, that Britain would be better off as part of the Eurozone. Back in February this year Stephens penned a remarkable column, under the headline "Britain would have fared better in the euro."[114]

Peter Sutherland was one of the most powerful proponents of the single currency. The former chairman of BP and eurocrat retains

---

[113] The Politics Show, BBC, 26 June 2011.

[114] *Financial Times*, 14 February 2011.

his optimism. This is what he told students at the opening of Kemmy Business School at the University of Limerick:[115]

> There are many commentating on the present crisis who have absolutely no idea what they are talking about, which is creating a culture of despair. People forget that there are things we do exceedingly well. Our youth are looked upon very well internationally, which is important in the global market. Employment is currently at 2002 levels, 80% higher than the level in 1992.

Many of these advocates of the single currency seem to have been suffering from a form of cognitive dissonance. This is a condition defined by psychologists as the mental perturbation that takes place when people holding strongly held beliefs are presented with powerful evidence that their assumptions are wrong. The economics writer Will Hutton is an especially curious example of this phenomenon. Like Philip Stephens, he continues in the face of catastrophe to believe in the benefits of the euro, as his recent article "Even now, the European project remains a noble one. Let's join in."[116]

On the other hand, Will Hutton is a diehard opponent of what he views as Chancellor George Osborne's tough budget measures, maintaining from a Keynesian perspective they will lead to economic disaster.[117] Will Hutton has one thing going for him. Unlike so many of his fellow pro-Euro supporters, he argues with

---

[115] Quoted in Colum Coomey, "Culture of Despair", *Limerick Post*, 11 November 2010.

[116] *Observer*, 24 July 2011.

[117] See, for example, "The Coalition is taking a huge gamble with the economy," *Observer*, 24 October 2010.

courtesy and treats his opponents with respect. He tends not to misrepresent their position or to spray out offensive personal insults.

But Hutton is trying to have it both ways. The cruel fact is that countries like Greece, Ireland, Spain and Portugal have been condemned to far worse austerity than Britain, precisely because of their membership of the Eurozone. It is the single currency in which Hutton so fervently believes that has brought up such terrible austerity across much of the European continent – and our own cuts would have been far worse had Britain taken his advice and joined. Hutton's position is, to put the matter bluntly, an intellectual shambles.

Yet at least he has the courage and conviction to continue to speak out and defend his position. Other pro-Euro columnists have retreated into silence. Consider the case of Andrew Rawnsley, as we have seen so noisily contemptuous about the euro-sceptics and so gung-ho about the single currency a decade ago. Rawnsley writes a weekly column for the *Observer* which covers the entire political waterfront. But over the last 18 months, one subject has been off the menu. Even though the Euro has been one of the biggest stories of the past two years, Rawnsley has avoided the subject. Not a single one of the columns written by Andrew Rawnsley between 1 January 2010 and the middle of September 2011 addresses the Euro.

The same applies to David Aaronovitch. A decade ago this columnist loved to trash the moral and personal character of euro-sceptics, while vigorously promoting the merits of the single currency. Not any more. Aaronovitch had written some 49 columns for the *Times* in 2011 by the time this pamphlet went to the printers in mid September, not a single one dealt with the Eurocrisis. In 2010, not one of Aaronovitch's 70-plus articles for the *Times* addressed the collapse of the euro.

Writers such as Rawnsley and Aaronovitch are open to the charge of cowardice. They should either admit they got it wrong, or come out and state why their position remains the same. Aaronovitch claimed in 2007 that he had been a dispassionate observer of the argument of the Euro, asserting:[118]

> "Europe (in the way 'Europe' has come to be used in media discourse) has never excited me that much...the stormy enthusiasms of the Phile and Phobes for their federal states or their magically separate nation states have seemed abstract and distant."

This relatively recent claim by Aaronovitch that he was a disinterested observer is, however, contradicted by the facts. The truth is that Aaronovitch was a Euro partisan who again and again brutally misrepresented the euro-sceptic cause, while supporting the single currency.

Owning up

Some credit goes to those who have changed their mind, and admitted as much. Danny Alexander, chief secretary to the Treasury, now acknowledges that joining the single currency would have been a mistake. He told a fringe meeting at the 2010 annual Liberal Democrat Party Conference:[119]

> In the current economic circumstances I'm relieved that we are not in the euro... I think that the flexibilities that we have as an economy are helping our economy to recover.

---

[118] *Times*, 26 June 2007.

[119] As reported on BBC News Online (http://www.bbc.co.uk/news/uk-politics-11380431), accessed 27 May 2011.

Coming from an individual who, as communications director of the Britain in Europe movement, dedicated five years of his life pressing for British entry to the Eurozone, this is a heartwarming and gracious concession. However too few of Danny Alexander's colleagues at Westminster have mirrored his honesty.

The *FT* columnist Wolfgang Munchau also commands respect. For many years he was one of the keenest enthusiasts for the single currency. As late as September 2006 he declared:

> I expect that Eurozone to be exceptionally stable in the long run... make no mistake, the Eurozone is here to stay.

Four years later, Munchau had performed his acrobatics. 'Whichever scenario you choose," wrote the *Financial Times* columnist in March last year, "the Euro is going to be weak."[120] Again, such candour has been all too rare among political and economic writers.

What to do about the BBC

As demonstrated above, the BBC news and current affairs operation lost its sense of fair-mindedness when it came to the single currency. It became in effect a partisan player in a great national debate – all the more insidiously effective because of its pretence at neutrality. Indeed senior figures at the BBC are now coming forward to admit that something was terribly wrong.

For example, Rod Liddle was editor of the Today programme from 1998 to 2002. This is what Liddle now says:

---

[120] "Rest assured, the Eurozone will prove its durability", *Financial Times*, 24 September 2006 and "Why the Euro will continue to weaken", *Financial Times*, 7 March 2010: both quotes courtesy of Open Europe research.

The whole ethos of the BBC and all of the staff was that euro-sceptics were xenophobes and Little Englanders and there was an end of it. The Euro would come up at a meeting and everybody would just burst out laughing about the euro-sceptics. Beyond all doubt the BBC was institutionally in favour of the single currency. That was the BBC position – of that there is no doubt at all.

But this BBC approval, adds Liddle, went way beyond the euro. He recalls:[121]

While I was editor of the Today programme I was often at war with the BBC Brussels office. You just never get those stories of waste, profligacy and corruption at Brussels out of them.

To its credit, the BBC now acknowledges that there has been a major problem. Two reports have been commissioned over the past few years: they concur that something went wrong.[122] The most powerful of these was the report carried out by Lord Wilson, the former cabinet secretary, and published in 2005. Its findings were devastating, all the more so when one considers that it was written by a long-term Whitehall insider, used to restrained and discreet language.

Wilson said that there was a "serious problem" in the BBC coverage of the European Union, lethally adding that:

---

[121] Ibid.

[122] In particular see the Wilson report of January 2005, available online at http://www.bbcgovernorsarchive.co.uk/docs/rev_eu_coverage.html, and the 2007 BBC Trust report on impartiality by John Bridcut at www.johnbridcut.com/documents/seesaw_to_wagon_wheel_report.pdf

Although the BBC wishes to be impartial in its news coverage of the EU it is not succeeding.

Lord Wilson found that the problem had spread across all levels of the BBC: "senior managers appear insufficiently self-critical about standards of impartiality". He added that "this attitude appears to have filtered through to producers, reporters and presenters in the front line." Lord Wilson found that there was "no evidence of any systematic monitoring to ensure that all shades of significant opinion are fairly represented." He also observed a phenomenon which is instantly recognisable to anyone who has ever attempted to raise BBC bias with a BBC producer or presenter: "a resistance to accepting external evidence." Lord Wilson demanded "urgent action" to redress these failings. There is very little evidence, however, that much has changed.

So there is still cause for enormous concern about the BBC and its coverage of the EU. This is an urgent problem, as it looks all too likely that a new treaty will be needed soon as a result of the euro-debacle if it is to survive. This would require Britain's signature – and very likely a referendum, something that would plunge the EU into the heart of our national politics.

The trouble is that the BBC in such a situation cannot be trusted. Its record is dreadful. Twice the European Union has been at the heart of our national debate. The first came in the referendum of 1975, the second in the national debate over the euro. On each occasion, the BBC lost all objectivity and became aligned to a partisan propaganda operation.

The scale of the problem can be seen just by studying membership of the BBC Trust. Today, both the chairman, Lord Patten and the vice chairman, Diane Coyle, were involved in the campaign to secure the single currency.[123] As we have seen, the latter used her position as economics writer for the *Independent* to make unfounded and prejudicial comments about eurosceptics. When Ms Coyle was appointed to her post earlier this year the outgoing BBC Trust chairman Michael Lyons praised her "wisdom, insight and consistent good humour."[124] None of these qualities were on display in her coverage of the single currency a decade ago.

The presence of Lord Patten and Diane Coyle as the two most senior figures on the BBC Trust is unacceptable, especially in the light of the corporation's disastrous past record of bias and prejudice. The board of the BBC Trust must be radically reconstituted.

Ten more lessons
What else can be learnt?

Lesson 1. Conventional wisdom is very often wrong
This does not just apply to the single currency – a cause which was long equated in the public sphere with moderation and sanity. It is important to reflect that many of the beliefs that were held most fervently ten years ago have now been turned on their head. Ten years ago, those who raised the issue of

---

[123] In his Chatham Lecture at Oxford in 2000, Chris Patten said: "Yet 'sovereignty' in the sense of unfettered freedom of action, is a nonsense. A man, naked, hungry and alone in the middle of the Sahara desert is free in the sense that no-one can tell him what to do. He is sovereign, then. But he is also doomed. It is often preferable to accept constraints on freedom of action in order to achieve some other benefit."

[124] "Diane Coyle named BBC Trust vice-chairman", *Guardian*, 24 March 2011.

immigration invited the ugly charge of racism. Now almost all mainstream politicians accept that it is an issue of serious public concern. Similarly anyone (such as Oliver Letwin when he was shadow Treasury spokesman) who suggested cuts to public spending came close to ostracism from public life. It is now clear that the warnings from Mr Letwin and others were all too realistic and far-sighted.

So we should always be careful to give space in the public square for ideas that challenge and affront us. Climate change is an example. Today it has entered official orthodoxy and has become hard to challenge. The experience of the single currency debate ten years ago does not prove those who challenge the climate change proposition are right. But it does suggest that they ought to be heard with respect.

Lesson 2. Cherish eccentricity

Study of the public discourse shows often pro-Euro propagandists questioned the sanity of their opponents, declaring them "mad" or "deranged." Many governing élites use this tactic, marginalising their critics by labelling them cranks. History has shown the opposite – it is the single currency supporters who were the cranks, while the euro-sceptics have been vindicated as sane.

Lesson 3. Be suspicious of cross-party alliances

Twelve years ago Labour, Tory and Liberal Democrats came together in the same platform to launch the Britain in Europe campaign. The grandees of all parties – Tony Blair, Ken Clarke, Michael Heseltine and Charles Kennedy – were there. Blair labelled William Hague's warning about the Euro 'shrill'. But history has shown that it was Tony Blair and the Britain in Europe campaign who were shrill.

It should not be forgotten that the two most disastrous British enterprises in recent history have been launched with cross-party support – the invasion of Iraq in 2003 (though without the Liberal Democrats) and entry to the Exchange Rate Mechanism in 1990. Today Britain is governed by a Coalition embracing the Tories, the Lib Dems, and (unofficially) the Blairite wing of Labour. This establishment sanction should not be used to infer that the Government's policies are sensible. Again and again it is those lonely and cussed figures who stand outside the establishment orthodoxy who get vindicated over time.

Lesson 4. The deceitful tactics of the Euro supporters were all too typical

When Britain signed up to what was then the Common Market in 1973, voters had been told that we were entering a trading area, and there was no reason to fear for national sovereignty and independence.[125] Later, when the single currency was introduced, similar false promises were made. We were told that the Eurozone would give us unprecedented economic and financial stability, that there was no need for further political integration, that economic collapse loomed unless we signed up to the euro, and that loss of national control over interest rates and exchange rates would not matter because European economies would converge. We were told that Britain would take a huge risk by staying out of the euro. We were not warned (except by the despised euro-sceptics) how dangerous membership would turn out to be.

---

[125] Prime Minister Edward Heath notoriously stated in a TV broadcast in 1973 that "there are some in this country who fear that in going into Europe we shall in some way sacrifice independence and sovereignty. These fears, I need hardly say, are completely unjustified."

The supporters of the single currency did not simply make a terrible error: they deceived us (and doubtless themselves) as well. Some members of the euro-élite have been honest enough to admit this. Herman Van Rompuy, President of the European Council, noted last year that:[126]

> We are clearly confronted with a tension within the system, the ill-famous dilemma of being a monetary union and a full-fledged economic and political union. The tension has been there since the single currency was created. However, the general public was not really made aware of it.

Lesson 5. Watch out as the euro-élite uses the same tactics
Even today, yet more misleading statements are being made as the EU battles to save the Eurozone.

We were told that there could be no financial bail-outs of embattled member states – there have been three so far.

We were told they were illegal – retrospective legislation is being introduced to change this.

We were told there could be no fiscal transfers between member states – the European Central Bank (ECB) in Frankfurt, as it provides tens of billions of liquidity to bankrupt peripheral economies, is now turning into a mechanism for quiet fiscal transfer, ultimately at the cost of the EU taxpayer.

We were told that the ECB President Jean-Claude Trichet would "defend the European Central Bank's independence under any

---

[126] "Ordinary people were misled over impact of the euro, says Herman Van Rompuy", *Daily Telegraph*, 26 May 2010.

circumstance and with all my strength".[127] This promise proved futile and he and his bank have both been captured by the big EU politicians. As a result the balance sheet of his bank is now in ruins. Like ECB independence, it has become a fiction, since the ECB marks at or near to book value its vast holdings of near worthless Greek, Irish and Portuguese debt.

Lesson 6. Karl Marx was right – economics trumps politics
At bottom, the single currency was driven by a single and unbreakable conviction: that political will can overcome economic reality. But history demonstrates that, while economic facts can sometimes be held in abeyance thanks to political manipulation, ultimately the power of economics will prevail.

Lesson 7. The pro-Euro advocates lack any social compassion
Left-wing critics loved to upbraid Margaret Thatcher for the "sado-monetarism" of the 1980s. Yet these self-same critics seem prepared to sanction, in the name of the single currency, the degradation of entire economies. Their monetary policies have led directly to 46% youth unemployment in Spain,[128] and the eradication of the Greek industrial base. Margaret Thatcher's monetarism in the 1980s never anywhere came near this fanaticism and contempt for ordinary people. Indeed, the austerity of Thatcherite economics counted for nothing compared to the dogmatism and blinkered ideology of the EU political class as it punishes out of line and failing member states.

---

[127] "Trichet: difenderò l'indipendenza della BCE", *Corriere della Sera*, 11 July 2007.

[128] "The jobless young: left behind", *Economist*, 10 September 2011.

Lesson 8. The Conservatives never were the real nasty party

Our study of the rhetorical techniques of the pro-Euro advocates raises a very important question: was the idea that the Conservatives were 'nasty' ever really true? Or was this 'nastiness' in large part a New Labour narrative, brilliantly sold by spin-doctors to a complicit media? There are certainly areas where the late 20th century Conservatives were out of touch with the age – most notably on social issues like gay rights. But it was New Labour which perfected the politics of personal destruction, with its culture of smear, its mockery of decent and public-spirited people and contempt for intellectual integrity. The ugly and unscrupulous methods used by the advocates of the single currency were a manifestation of this debased public discourse.

Lesson 9. It is time for the Euro supporters to apologise

There is a strand in British public life that has long urged greater integration between the UK and the EU. The late Roy Jenkins belonged to this honourable (though in our view wrong-headed) tradition. So do contemporary politicians from all of our major parties ranging from Ken Clarke and Michael Heseltine to David Miliband and Peter Mandelson to Nick Clegg and Danny Alexander.

It is of course essential for our democracy that this pro-Euro point of view should be heard. But first of all we are all entitled to an explanation from the Euro supporters about why they tried to press Britain to take the calamitous path of joining the single currency.

If they now accept they were wrong, they should say so, and explain why it was that they came to be so mistaken on the greatest economic issue of our age. If they still believe they were right, and they stand by their arguments, they should come out and say so publicly and defend themselves.

Silence is, however, unacceptable. Their cowardice means that they no longer have a moral right to enter into the great debate that is brewing about the future of Britain within the EU. Here are some of the names from whom we are waiting to hear: Lord Marshall, Adair Turner, Michael Heseltine, Neil Kinnock, Chris Huhne and Nick Clegg.

And it must be said that from some members of the pro-Euro camp we need more than just an admission of error. Those who lied, cheated and misrepresented the motives of their euro-sceptic opponents owe an apology to those they insulted. Top of the list comes Tony Blair, who during his party conference speech of 1999 implied that Conservative euro-scepticism stood in the foul tradition of South African racism. There can be no place in our national debate for this kind of cheap and debased argument, which sadly poisoned so much of the British debate over the single currency.

Lesson 10. It is time to celebrate those who fought to save sterling

Had the British political class succeeded in their plan to sign the UK up to the single currency, they would have ruined our economy and destroyed our national independence. There are many courageous public women and men who deserve their share of the credit. In the end, however, we must recognise that if the politicians had had their way we would have gone in. It was the British people who, thank God, blocked it.

APPENDIX ONE

A SELECTION OF SCARE STORIES

Boycotting Euro could cost 3m jobs and £6bn
Daily Express, 23 February, 1999
The National Institute of Economic and Social Research forecasts that 40,000 City jobs will disappear over the next 10 years if Britain follows an isolationist course...

Economist Garry Young said: "By 2010 the output of the City could be 20 per cent lower than now."

Euro campaigners clash on jobs: Lord Marshall says investors will pull out of Britain but sceptics ridicule claims
Guardian, 30 June, 1999
Up to a million jobs could be lost if Britain rejects the single currency, business and union leaders of the pro-Euro campaign, Britain in Europe, warned yesterday.

Lord Marshall, chairman of the campaign, joined forces with Sir Ken Jackson, the engineering union leader, to claim that inward investors would pull out of Britain, putting at risk actual and potential jobs.

Quitting EU 'would hurt inward investment'
Financial Times, 18 February, 2000
Inward investment in manufacturing would be cut by a third if Britain withdrew from the European Union, according to the National Institute of Economic and Social Research.

Eight million jobs 'would be lost if Britain quit EU'
The Independent, 18 February, 2000
EIGHT MILLION jobs would be lost if Britain were to leave the European Union, according to a study by academics to be published next week.

The report by the National Institute of Economic and Social Research will be seized on by Tony Blair and other ministers as they launch a campaign to turn the Euro-sceptic tide amongst the British public...

"The country is tipping further and further towards the precipice," one pro-EU campaigner said yesterday. "We have got to draw a line in the sand and say 'thus far, no further.' At the bottom of this slippery slope, we would end up with eight million people out of work."

Blair backs warning on jobs toll of quitting EU
Daily Express, 19 February, 2000
TONY Blair last night backed warnings that millions of jobs would be in jeopardy if Britain were to pull out of the EU.

Downing Street moved swiftly after Daily Express revealed research reported to the Britain in Europe (BiE) campaign group, suggesting eight million jobs could go.

"We have always been clear that millions of British jobs depend on Europe and that many more would be indirectly affected were we to withdraw from the EU," said a Downing Street spokesman.

'Adopt Euro or lose jobs'
Daily Mirror, 29 December, 2001
UNION boss John Monks yesterday said Labour dithering over the Euro will cost 150,000 jobs.

Euro-lag 'hits us for pounds 4.5bn a year'
Daily Mirror, 21 December, 2001
BRITAIN will have missed the boat if it doesn't join the Euro within two-and-a-half years, British Airways' chairman Lord Marshall warned yesterday.

Speaking exclusively to *The Mirror*, the peer urged the Government to wake up to the pounds £4.5 billion sum that UK business loses each year because of the strength of the pound.

"I really hope that in the next two-and-a-half years we will have decided to join the euro. It costs UK exporters billions while we stay outside the single currency."

Euro delay 'puts 2,000 jobs at risk in Blair seat'
Times, 11 July, 2002
ONE of the biggest employers in Tony Blair's constituency is threatening to move overseas if Britain does not sign up to the euro.

Black & Decker executives have told the Prime Minister that up to 2,000 jobs in Spennymoor, on the border of his Sedgefield seat, are at risk partly because of uncertainty over the Government's policy on the single currency.[129]

---

[129] According to the *Northern Echo*: "Black & Decker shed almost 1,000 jobs at Spennymoor in 2003 to reduce costs by moving some production to Eastern Europe." So while jobs were cut, it seems that this was more to do with the lower labour costs of Eastern Europe.

APPENDIX TWO

THE ECONOMIC REALITY

Again and again, warnings from the pro-single currency propagandists that the UK would not survive outside the Eurozone proved wide of the mark. Ten years on from the debate, it is possible to make a provisional judgement. While there have been areas of economic performance where the Eurozone has performed better, in general the UK economy has greatly outperformed on four key measures

1. Unemployment

Unemployment for the Euro area as a whole has fluctuated (mainly due to different countries joining throughout the period). But unemployment in the Euro area in December 2010 was 10.1%, compared with 7.8% in the UK.

The Euro area's record low rate of unemployment was 7.9% in April 2001 (at the time UK unemployment was 4.8%). The UK's lowest rate over the last ten years has been around 3% lower than the Euro area's lowest.[130] Despite the doomsday

---

[130] Harmonised unemployment rates (monthly data). Eurostat, *Unemployment Rate by ILO definition.*

predictions about lost jobs in financial services, the UK now has 35,000 more people working in financial services than at the start of 1999.[131] On the other hand, Eurostat data does suggest that the UK has lost manufacturing jobs at a faster rate than the Euro area. The UK now only has 63% of the manufacturing jobs it had in 2000, compared with 86% retention in the current 17 Euro area countries.

2. Growth

The UK enjoyed better real GDP growth than the current Euro area countries between 2000 and 2010. Real GDP growth was higher in the UK than in the euro-17 in six of the eight years prior to the financial crisis in 2008.[132] It should again be noted, however, the UK was adversely affected by the recession due to the dominance of financial services and the state of the public finances and has had lower real GDP growth in the past two years, in part due to much higher inflation.

3. Inflation

Both the Eurozone and the UK were effective in keeping inflation at low levels until the onset of recession in 2008. Between 2000 and 2005, the UK had lower rates of HICP inflation than the Eurozone area in every year, and between 2005 and 2008 the rates were almost identical. In the last two years, inflation has been significantly higher in the UK, however.[133]

---

[131] 1.146m people in 2011 Q1, compared with 1.111m in 1999 Q1.

[132] http://epp.eurostat.ec.europa.eu/tgm/table.do?tab=table&plugin=1&language=en&pcode=tsieb020

[133] All items HICP (annual average rate of change).

4. Direct investment inflows

One of the main criticisms of the UK's decision not to join the Euro was the potential for the loss of inflows of foreign direct investment.

OECD data on inflows shows that between 2000 and 2008 the UK has received $873bn in inflows, compared with France and Germany, who received $576bn and $486bn respectively. In 2007, the UK received $183bn – which was more than the sum of both France and Germany ($160bn) that year.[134] Data from the last available year, 2008, shows that the UK obtained $96bn of FDI, compared with $97bn to France and just $25bn to Germany.

---

[134] OECD International Direct Investment (inflows $).

AFTERWORD

Soon after embarking on the research for this pamphlet, we became aware that a significant part of our work had already been carried out for us. When the Euro debate was at its height at the turn of the century, the *Sunday Telegraph* journalist Christopher Booker was already writing about the dishonesty shown by the pro-Euro camp, and the complicity of the BBC and the CBI. We have cheerfully plundered Booker's valuable and far-sighted investigations, and to him we owe many thanks.

Our second debt is to Lord Pearson of Rannoch. Like Booker, Pearson was very troubled about the partial BBC coverage. This led him to start Minotaur Media Tracking, run by David Keighley, a former head of current affairs at the BBC. Keighley monitored hundreds of hours of BBC news and current affairs coverage. It goes without saying that BBC executives have tried from time to time tried to discredit Keighley, but they have not succeeded. As far as we have been able to determine, his professionalism is beyond doubt.

It is hard to praise too strongly this work by Minotaur. From what we have seen, it appears rigorous, painstaking, fair-minded and thorough. Furthermore, but for Minotaur it would have been impossible to reach a judgement about the BBC coverage:

there would have been few records to inspect. Minotaur has carried out – in addition to everything else – a valuable service to history.

Support for the research and publication of this study was given by Nigel Vinson and the Politics & Economics Research Trust, the Institute for Policy Research, Andrew Hamilton & Company, Chartered Accountants, Alex Hammond Chambers, Artemis Investment Management LLP, Greenfield Marquees Ltd and Hamilton Financial (Scotland) Ltd, Investment Advisors.

We would like to thank the Open Europe think tank and in particular Mats Persson and Raoul Ruparel. They have been a constant source of enlightenment and information over recent years, and we have drawn a number of relevant quotations from their brilliantly researched pamphlet *They Said It: How the European Elite Got It Wrong On The Euro.*

We would like to acknowledge the contribution made to this pamphlet by Patrick Halling and Amanda Drugnik. They have both carried out invaluable research. We would also like to thank Jonathan Collett, Director of the Bruges Group from 1993 to 2001, for his comments on the text. Ryan Bourne of the Centre for Policy Studies did an excellent job preparing Appendix 2. We are also intensely grateful to Tom Greeves who once again was of immense use as a fact-checker and analyst. Peter Oborne would also like to express his thanks to all those at the *Daily Telegraph,* which has been consistently right on this great issue, for their advice and support.

INDEX

BECOME AN ASSOCIATE OF
THE CENTRE FOR POLICY STUDIES

The Centre for Policy Studies is one of Britain's best-known and most respected think tanks. Independent from all political parties and pressure groups, it consistently advocates a distinctive case for smaller, less intrusive government, with greater freedom and responsibility for individuals, families, business and the voluntary sector.

Through our Associate Membership scheme, we welcome supporters who take an interest in our work. Associate Membership is available for £100 a year. Becoming an Associate will entitle you to:

- all CPS publications produced in a 12-month period
- invitations to lectures and conferences
- advance notice by e-mail of our publications, briefing papers and invitations to special events

For more details, please write or telephone to:
The Secretary
Centre for Policy Studies
57 Tufton Street, London SW1P 3QL
Tel: 020 7222 4488
Fax: 020 7222 4388
e-mail: mail@cps.org.uk
Website: www.cps.org.uk

Centre for Policy Studies

SOME RECENT PUBLICATIONS

The £100 billion negotiations by Michael Johnson
"The unions' negotiating position is that Lord Hutton's calculations showed that public sector pensions are affordable. But Johnson points out that this was based on implementing changes still to be agreed. And he claims, 'Lord Hutton's assumptions for growth, productivity and public sector job growth – which make public sector pensions appear more affordable – look increasingly optimistic.'" – Lourna Bourke, *Citywire*

Something can be done by Affan Burki and Tom Burkard
"Soldiers 'should run schools in crackdown on indiscipline'" – headline in *The Daily Telegraph*

Look back from the future: a radical path to growth and prosperity by Norman Blackwell
"We need to look back from the future to assess what government policies are needed to boost productivity" – headline on *Conservative Home*

Give us our fair shares: how to get best value for taxpayers from reprivatising the banks by James Conway, Toby Fenwick and Michael O'Connor
"The principle of wider share ownership of the banks is sound. It would pay back taxpayers for the pain suffered owing to irresponsible lending by the banks and change the way the public think about banks" – leading article in *The Times*

Five fiscal fallacies by Tim Morgan
"Anyone who wants to understand what has happened could do worse than read a brilliantly lucid and illuminating pamphlet written by the economist Tim Morgan, published by the Centre for Policy Studies" – Stephen Glover in *The Daily Mail*